Hands-On Machine Learning with IBM Watson

Leverage IBM Watson to implement machine learning
techniques and algorithms using Python

James D. Miller

BIRMINGHAM - MUMBAI

Hands-On Machine Learning with IBM Watson

Commissioning Editor: Sunith Shetty
Acquisition Editor: Yogesh Deokar
Content Development Editor: Athikho Sapuni Rishana
Technical Editor: Vibhuti Gawde
Copy Editor: Safis Editing
Project Coordinator: Kirti Pisat
Proofreader: Safis Editing
Indexer: Priyanka Dhadke
Graphics: Jisha Chirayil
Production Coordinator: Arvindkumar Gupta

First published: March 2019

Production reference: 1280319

Published by Packt Publishing Ltd.
Livery Place
35 Livery Street
Birmingham
B3 2PB, UK.

ISBN 978-1-78961-185-4

www.packtpub.com

`mapt.io`

Mapt is an online digital library that gives you full access to over 5,000 books and videos, as well as industry leading tools to help you plan your personal development and advance your career. For more information, please visit our website.

Why subscribe?

- Spend less time learning and more time coding with practical eBooks and Videos from over 4,000 industry professionals

- Improve your learning with Skill Plans built especially for you

- Get a free eBook or video every month

- Mapt is fully searchable

- Copy and paste, print, and bookmark content

Packt.com

Did you know that Packt offers eBook versions of every book published, with PDF and ePub files available? You can upgrade to the eBook version at `www.packt.com` and as a print book customer, you are entitled to a discount on the eBook copy. Get in touch with us at `customercare@packtpub.com` for more details.

At `www.packt.com`, you can also read a collection of free technical articles, sign up for a range of free newsletters, and receive exclusive discounts and offers on Packt books and eBooks.

Contributors

About the author

James D. Miller is an innovator and accomplished senior project lead and solution architect with 37 years' experience of extensive design and development across multiple platforms and technologies. Roles include leveraging his consulting experience to provide hands-on leadership in all phases of advanced analytics and related technology projects, providing recommendations for process improvement, report accuracy, the adoption of disruptive technologies, enablement, and insight identification. He has also written a number of books, including *Statistics for Data Science*; *Mastering Predictive Analytics with R, Second Edition*; *Big Data Visualization*; *Learning Watson Analytics*; and many more.

This book is dedicated to the memory of my father, James A. Miller Jr. and as always, my guardian angel and wife Nanette.

About the reviewer

Mayur Ravindra Narkhede is a researcher with BTech in computer science and an MTech in CSE, specializing in AI. He is a data scientist with core experience in building automated end-to-end solutions, and is proficient at applying technology, AI, ML, data mining, and design thinking to improve business functions with growth profitability. He has worked on multiple advanced solutions for the oil and gas sector, utilities, financial services, road traffic and transport, life science, and big data platforms for asset-intensive industries. He has also played a key role in setting up a data science and big data lab for research and development work. He likes to play badminton, carom, billiards, and goes trekking occasionally, and loves to travel.

Packt is searching for authors like you

If you're interested in becoming an author for Packt, please visit authors.packtpub.com and apply today. We have worked with thousands of developers and tech professionals, just like you, to help them share their insight with the global tech community. You can make a general application, apply for a specific hot topic that we are recruiting an author for, or submit your own idea.

Table of Contents

Preface

This book serves as a complete guide to becoming well-versed in machine learning on IBM Cloud using Python. You will learn how to build complete machine learning solutions, focusing on the role of data representation and feature extraction.

This book starts with supervised and unsupervised machine learning concepts, including an overview of IBM Cloud and the Watson Machine Learning service. You will learn how to run various techniques, such as k-means clustering, KNN, time series prediction, visual recognition, and text-to-speech in IBM Cloud by means of real-world examples. You will learn how to create a Spark pipeline in Watson Studio. The book will also guide you in terms of deep learning and neural network principles on IBM Cloud with TensorFlow. You will learn how to build chatbots using NLP techniques. Later, you will cover three powerful case studies – the facial expression classification platform, the automated classification of lithofacies, and the multibiometric identity authentication platform – with a view to becoming well-versed in the methodologies.

By the end of the book, you will be well-positioned to build efficient machine learning solutions on IBM Cloud. You will also be well-equipped with real-world examples to draw insights from the data at hand.

Who this book is for

This book is aimed at data scientists and machine learning engineers who would like to get introduced to IBM Cloud and its machine learning services using practical examples.

What this book covers

Chapter 1, *Introduction to IBM Cloud*, provides a brief introduction to the IBM cloud platform and the machine learning service. Moreover, this chapter provides detailed instructions on how to set up data science and machine learning development environments on IBM Cloud. Finally, it conclude in with an example for loading and visualizing data.

Chapter 2, *Feature Extraction – A Bag of Tricks*, provides a hands-on guide to extraction and the selection of features from real-life data, with an emphasis on the fact that practical machine learning systems are all about proper feature engineering. This chapter demonstrates best practices for feeding data to your machine learning algorithms. Moreover, it shows how to remove redundant data that negatively impacts the performance of your machine learning system. This chapter also introduces strategies for combining data from different sources.

Chapter 3, *Supervised Machine Learning Models for Your Data*, acts as the backbone of the entire book. It provides a tour of the machine learning paradigm, with a focus on famous approaches and algorithms. This chapter starts by providing a practical background to model evaluation, model selection, and algorithm selection in machine learning. Then it covers supervised learning, and discusses machine learning algorithms for regression problems. By the end of the chapter, you should be able to select proper supervised machine learning models for the data at hand.

Chapter 4, *Implementing Unsupervised Algorithms*, is the sequel to the tour of the machine learning paradigm that began in Chapter 2, *Feature Extraction – A Bag of Tricks*. This chapter covers unsupervised learning and semi-supervised learning. Moreover, it discusses famous clustering algorithms, before concluding with a discussion of online versus batch learning.

Chapter 5, *Machine Learning Workouts on IBM Cloud*, provides several examples that are carefully designed to uncover the power of Python as a machine learning programming language of choice and the power of the machine learning service on the IBM Watson Studio platform. This chapter will enable you to practice proper feature engineering. Moreover, you will be able to run supervised (classification) and unsupervised (clustering) techniques in the cloud. Furthermore, this chapter will guide you on implementing time series prediction algorithms. Finally, it concludes with visual recognition examples.

Chapter 6, *Using Spark with IBM Watson Studio*, provides guidelines for creating a Spark machine learning pipeline within IBM Watson Studio.

Chapter 7, *Deep Learning Using TensorFlow on IBM Cloud*, provides an introduction to deep learning and neural networks on IBM Cloud. An overview of the use of TensorFlow on the cloud will also be provided. This chapter is designed to balance theory and practical implementation.

Chapter 8, *Creating a Facial Expression Platform on IBM Cloud*, covers a complete, cloud-based facial expression classification solution using deep learning. It implements a simple, yet efficient, neural network model using TensorFlow and the machine learning service on Watson Studio. This chapter demonstrates an end-to-end solution for a complex machine learning task.

Chapter 9, *The Automated Classification of Lithofacies Formation Using ML*, demonstrates a cloud-based machine learning system for identifying lithofacies based on well-log measurements. This is a crucial step in drilling applications. First, we will begin by introducing the problem and the dataset. Then we will explain the types of post-processing needed for such cases. Finally, the complete solution is built using the machine learning service on the Watson platform.

Chapter 10, *Building a Cloud-Based Multibiometric Identity Authentication Platform*, guides the reader on how to build a complete cloud-based human identification system using biometric traits. This chapter begins by introducing the problem and the datasets. Then it explains the types of post-processing needed for each biometric. Moreover, you will learn how to extract meaningful features. Learning and recognition will follow. Finally, you will practice multimodal data fusion.

Chapter 11, *Conclusion*, concludes the book with an overview of what has been covered. This chapter also sheds some light on some of the practical considerations related to developing machine learning systems on the cloud. Finally, the book concludes with further discussions on different routes the reader might consider to enhance their skills.

To get the most out of this book

A basic knowledge of Python and a limited understanding of machine learning will be beneficial.

Download the example code files

You can download the example code files for this book from your account at www.packt.com. If you purchased this book elsewhere, you can visit www.packt.com/support and register to have the files emailed directly to you.

You can download the code files by following these steps:

1. Log in or register at www.packt.com.
2. Select the **SUPPORT** tab.
3. Click on **Code Downloads & Errata**.
4. Enter the name of the book in the **Search** box and follow the onscreen instructions.

Once the file is downloaded, please make sure that you unzip or extract the folder using the latest version of:

- WinRAR/7-Zip for Windows
- Zipeg/iZip/UnRarX for Mac
- 7-Zip/PeaZip for Linux

The code bundle for the book is also hosted on GitHub at `https://github.com/PacktPublishing/Hands-On-Machine-Learning-with-IBM-Watson`. In case there's an update to the code, it will be updated on the existing GitHub repository.

We also have other code bundles from our rich catalog of books and videos available at `https://github.com/PacktPublishing/`. Check them out!

Download the color images

We also provide a PDF file that has color images of the screenshots/diagrams used in this book. You can download it here: `http://www.packtpub.com/sites/default/files/downloads/9781789611854_ColorImages.pdf`.

Conventions used

There are a number of text conventions used throughout this book.

`CodeInText`: Indicates code words in text, database table names, folder names, filenames, file extensions, pathnames, dummy URLs, user input, and Twitter handles. Here is an example: "The file we are using in this project (`combine.csv`) is a comma-delimited text file containing statistics on players who attended the NFL scouting combine."

A block of code is set as follows:

```
df_data_2.createOrReplaceTempView("station")
sqlDF = spark.sql("SELECT * FROM station where VALUE > 200")
sqlDF.show()
```

When we wish to draw your attention to a particular part of a code block, the relevant lines or items are set in bold:

```
[default]
exten => s,1,Dial(Zap/1|30)
exten => s,2,Voicemail(u100)
exten => s,102,Voicemail(b100)
exten => i,1,Voicemail(s0)
```

Bold: Indicates a new term, an important word, or words that you see on screen. For example, words in menus or dialog boxes appear in the text like this. Here is an example: "If you click on the blue **Cloud sign-up/log-in** link, you can create a free account (using your IBM ID) or log in (once you have set up your paid or free account)."

 Warnings or important notes appear like this.

 Tips and tricks appear like this.

Get in touch

Feedback from our readers is always welcome.

General feedback: If you have questions about any aspect of this book, mention the book title in the subject of your message and email us at customercare@packtpub.com.

Errata: Although we have taken every care to ensure the accuracy of our content, mistakes do happen. If you have found a mistake in this book, we would be grateful if you would report this to us. Please visit www.packt.com/submit-errata, selecting your book, clicking on the Errata Submission Form link, and entering the details.

Piracy: If you come across any illegal copies of our works in any form on the internet, we would be grateful if you would provide us with the location address or website name. Please contact us at copyright@packt.com with a link to the material.

If you are interested in becoming an author: If there is a topic that you have expertise in, and you are interested in either writing or contributing to a book, please visit authors.packtpub.com.

Reviews

Please leave a review. Once you have read and used this book, why not leave a review on the site that you purchased it from? Potential readers can then see and use your unbiased opinion to make purchase decisions, we at Packt can understand what you think about our products, and our authors can see your feedback on their book. Thank you!

For more information about Packt, please visit `packt.com`.

Section 1: Introduction and Foundation

This is an introduction to IBM Cloud and machine learning. This part of the book will help you in setting up the development environment and necessary APIs for the upcoming projects.

The following chapters will be covered in this section:

- Chapter 1, *Introduction to IBM Cloud*
- Chapter 2, *Feature Extraction – A Bag of Tricks*
- Chapter 3, *Supervised Machine Learning Models for Your Data*
- Chapter 4, *Implementing Unsupervised Algorithms*

Introduction to IBM Cloud

1

In this chapter, we will provide a brief introduction to the IBM Cloud platform and the services that it offers, such as **machine learning** (**ML**). Moreover, this chapter will provide detailed instructions on how to set up a data science and machine learning development environment on the IBM Cloud. Finally, we will conclude with a project example that involves loading and visualizing data.

We'll break down this first chapter into the following sections:

- Understanding IBM Cloud
- The IBM Cloud and Watson Machine Learning services
- Setting up the environment
- Data visualization tutorial

Understanding IBM Cloud

What can we say about the IBM Cloud environment? What makes it unique and so exciting? To start, the IBM Cloud platform (formerly known as **Bluemix**) actually combines **platform as a service** (**PaaS**) with **infrastructure as a service** (**IaaS**) and, in addition, offers a collection or catalog of cloud services that you can integrate with PaaS and IaaS to efficiently build individual, enterprise, or even global innovative applications.

Some other key points on the IBM Cloud (from a developer perspective) include the following:

- You can develop in what is called a **cloud without borders**, which means that you can connect private services to the public IBM Cloud services that are available from IBM
- You can expect to see a continuously growing number of services and runtime frameworks being added and becoming available to you

- You can take an idea from start, to development sandbox, to a globally distributed environment with the IBM Watson tools and services without having to make major investments
- You can test and adopt an extensive range of cloud services and capabilities from IBM, open source communities, and third-party developers
- You can control resources in real time as per the needs or workload demands change

There's much more we can do.

Prerequisites

Being a cloud-based environment, the IBM Cloud has no prerequisites to worry about, which makes getting it up and running pretty easy. All you really need is a web browser (see the documentation for the recommended versions) and a reasonable internet connection.

Optional, but recommended, is the **IBM Cloud Developer Toolset**. IBM touts this as a unified way to interact with your applications, containers, infrastructures, and other services. In this installation, you get the standalone IBM Cloud **command-line interface (CLI)**, plus various tools such as Git, Docker, Helm, kubectl, and curl, as well as the following IBM Cloud plugins:

- IBM Cloud Developer Tools plugin
- IBM Cloud Functions plugin
- IBM Cloud Container Registry plugin
- IBM Cloud Kubernetes Service plugin
- The sdk-gen plugin

 If you want to install both the IBM Cloud CLI and the other recommended plugins and tools for developing applications for IBM Cloud, follow the method described online here: https://console.bluemix.net/docs/cli/index.html#overview.

Accessing the IBM Cloud

Let's get started! To access the IBM Cloud, you can go to `https://www.ibm.com/cloud` where you will arrive at the **Cloud sign-up/log-in** page, which is shown in the following screenshot:

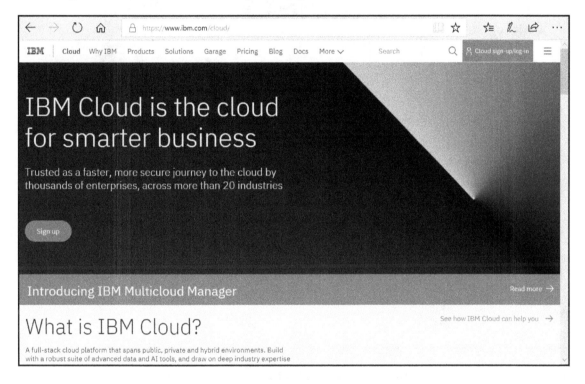

If you click on the blue **Cloud sign-up/log-in** link, you can create a free account (using your IBM ID) or log in (once you have set up your paid or free account).

After your ID has been authenticated, you will arrive at the IBM Cloud main page or the console, which is shown in the following screenshot:

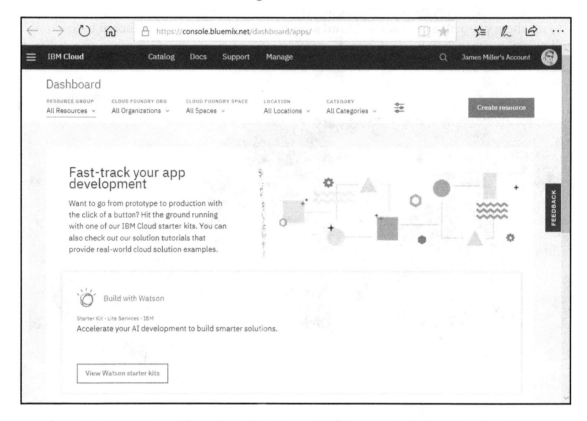

The **IBM Cloud console** is the user interface that you use to manage all of your IBM Cloud resources. When you access the console, you can manage your account, log in, access the documentation, access the catalog, view the pricing information, get support, or check the status of IBM Cloud components.

After you log in, the **menu bar** contains a Navigation Menu icon and additional links, depending on your account type.

From the console, you can perform the following tasks:

- Use the Navigation Menu icon to access all existing resources on your dashboard
- Use the **Catalog** link to create new resources
- Use the **Docs** link to access useful information about IBM Cloud

- From the **Support** menu, you can access information about what's new in IBM Cloud, the support center, options for adding and viewing tickets, and the status page
- From the **Manage** menu, you can access your account, billing and usage information, and security options
- Press the forward slash key (/) on your keyboard to navigate your cursor to the search field

Cloud resources

Through the IBM Cloud dashboard or console, you can view and work with **IBM Cloud resources** and **Cloud Foundry** service instances. We'll dive deeper into these in later chapters, but for now, you can think of a resource as anything that can be created, managed, and contained within a resource group. Some examples include apps, service instances, container clusters, storage volumes, and virtual servers.

In the following screenshot, you'll see the top portion of the console:

Rather than walking you through the entire list of functions and features here, we are going to focus on the areas of the cloud that will help jumpstart our ML project development. The IBM Cloud offers neat developer dashboards (accessible from the Navigate Menu icon in the upper left of the console page), each focusing on a different area of interest (such as **Watson**, **Security**, or **Finance**) or a digital channel (such as **Mobile** or **Web Apps**).

The menu list of developer dashboards is shown in the following screenshot:

Each developer dashboard provides various starter kits that are applicable to the dashboard's focus area, offering a consistent, intuitive workflow, which then helps you create a working app solution in minutes.

The IBM Cloud and Watson Machine Learning services

Selecting Watson from the list of starter kits offered opens the **Build with Watson** page, the upper portion of which is shown in the following screenshot:

This page is organized into sections, namely **Overview**, **Starter Kits**, **Watson Services**, **Developer Resources**, and **Apps**. If you click on **Watson Services**, then **Browse Services**, the current Watson-related services that are offered are presented as panels, as shown in the following screenshot:

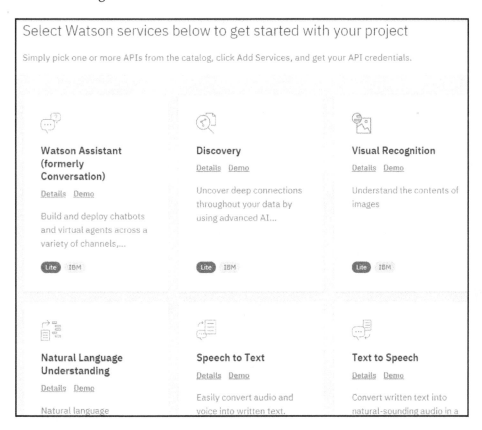

At this point, we need to find a service instance we want to use. To select a service offering, you can click on the panel that you are interested in (for example, **Machine Learning**). To make sure that this is the offering you want, you can click on **Details** and read through the service description, including its features list and other relevant information (as shown in the following screenshot) before clicking on **Create**:

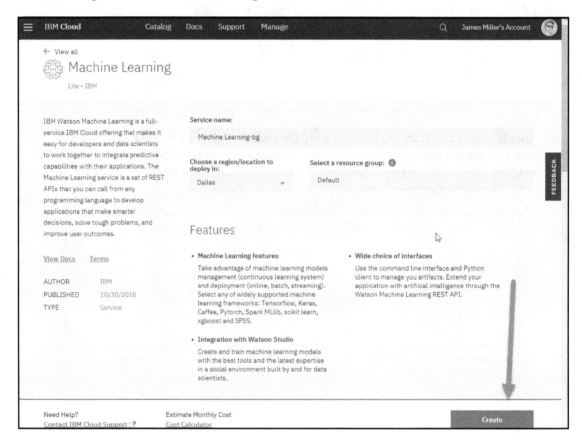

 Want more details? Don't forget to click on the **View Docs** link on the page.

Setting up the environment

To build Watson-based projects, you'll want to access the IBM Watson Studio.

 You'll access the IBM Watson Studio from the Cloud **Dashboard** menu (using the URL given in the preceding *Accessing the IBM Cloud* section).

IBM Watson Studio is an integrated environment designed to make it easy to develop, train, and manage models, as well as deploy AI-powered applications. You can use the neural network modeler and deep learning experiments in Watson Studio to solve the most challenging and computationally intensive problems with clarity and ease. You'll need your IBM ID to set this up.

There are currently three versions of Watson Studio, namely **Cloud**, **Desktop**, and **Local**, each offering a solution based on where you want to perform your work:

- **Watson Studio Cloud**: Your models reside in the IBM public cloud
- **Watson Studio Desktop**: Your models reside on your desktop
- **Watson Studio Local**: Your models reside either on your private local area network or on a private IBM cloud

In this book, we will initially focus on Watson Studio Cloud.

Watson Studio Cloud

Once the setup is done, you'll find that the Watson Studio Cloud format is similar to other IBM sites we've worked with (IBM Watson Analytics and the Cloud console, for example):

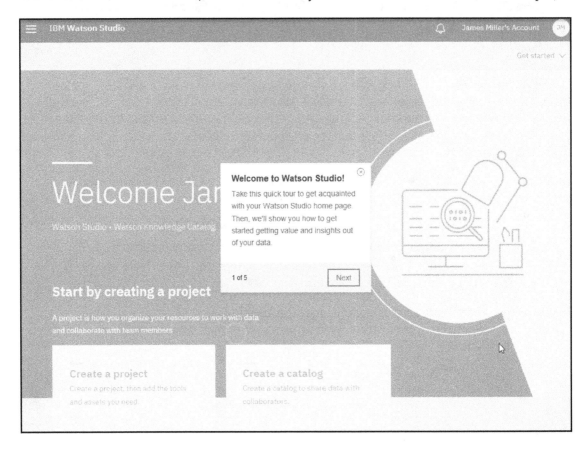

All of the versions of Watson Studio provide you with the environment and tools to solve your business problems by collaboratively working with data. You can choose the tools you need to analyze and visualize data, cleanse and shape data, ingest streaming data, or to create, train, and deploy ML models.

Watson Studio architecture and layout

The architecture of Watson Studio is centered around the concept of a project. A project is where you organize your resources and work with data. The most important resources in a project include collaborators (your users, categorized by security roles), data assets (these point to the data to be used in the project), and various analytical assets and tools (where you derive insights from data).

 Some interesting tools are provided, which we will touch on later in this book, such as the Streams Designer, the Data Refinery, RStudio, and so on. You can also bring in data and analytic assets from the IBM Watson Community.

You'll find that the Watson Studio main or home page (sometimes referred to as a panel rather than a page) is organized nicely into the following sections:

- A **Get started** section (shown in the previous screenshot) where you can click on panels to create a (new) project or catalog.
- A last or **Recently updated projects** section where you can see links to the projects you have access to or create new projects by clicking on **New Project**:

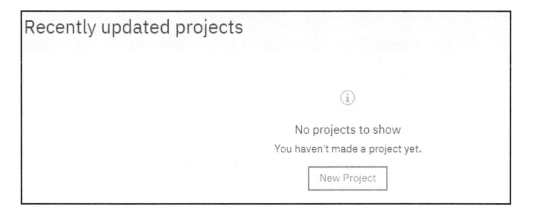

- A **Your catalogs** section, where you can see the links to the catalogs that you have access to; you can also create a new one:

 A catalog is where you organize your assets (for example, your data, data connections, and analysis) and collaborators.

- A **Watson services** section where you can see the list of active services and tools you have been using or add a new service:

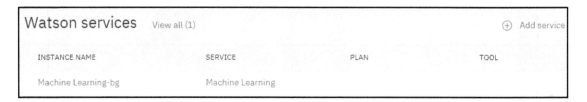

- Other sections include the **New in the community** section:

- You can also look at **Helpful links**:

Watson Studio simplifies the managing of service instances, collaborating with teammates, as well as designing, training, and deploying models. This topic is about getting set up to work with machine learning in Watson Studio.

To get set up to work with Watson Machine Learning without using Watson Studio, see this link: `https://dataplatform.cloud.ibm.com/docs/content/analyze-data/ml-setup.html`.

Establishing context

What we need to do before we set up a project is ask ourselves: do we want to create a new project or reuse an existing project? Next, do we want to create a new Watson Machine Learning service instance or reuse one we already have?

Setting up a new project

Simply put, to review what we already went over, to set up our first new project, we need to click on the **IBM Watson** link in the header area of the main page to navigate to the **IBM Watson Studio** home panel. We will then perform the following steps:

1. Click on **New Project**.

2. Choose a project type:
   - If you want to train complex neural networks using experiments, choose a **Deep Learning** project
   - For all other machine learning work, choose the **Modeler** project type

3. If you don't have any of the required services already, such as **Watson Machine Learning** and **IBM Cloud Object Storage**, new service instances are created.

At this point, we could dig further into each of the administrative areas of IBM Watson Studio, but the objective of this book is more outcome oriented and hands-on, so perhaps the best next step is to have a look at a small but concrete project, which we will do in the next section.

 Helpful key terms related to IBM Watson Machine Learning and IBM Watson Studio can be reviewed online at `https://dataplatform.cloud.ibm.com/docs/content/analyze-data/ml-terminology.html`.

Data visualization tutorial

Let's get started with a simple project!

As always, you begin any project with a statement of the project's objectives. In this project, the objective is to use a simple text file (`TripRuns.csv`), which contains results from a professional driving services organization, to show how easy it is to create a simple visual analytics dashboard with IBM Watson Studio.

 With an analytics dashboard, you can build sophisticated visualizations of analytics results, communicate insights based upon those results on the dashboard, and then easily share the dashboard with others. Cognos Dashboard Embedded uses the dashboard functionality from IBM Cognos Analytics. You can learn more about how to use the dashboard by visiting the following URL: `https://www.ibm.com/support/knowledgecenter/en/SSEP7J_11.0.0/com.ibm.swg.ba.cognos.ug_ca_dshb.doc/wa_dashboard_discoveryset_intro.html`.

Now that we have our project objective stated and clearly in mind, we need to follow these step-by-step instructions:

1. Click on **New Project**.
2. Next, click on the **Create a project** page. Choose a project starter (required services are provisioned automatically. You can add other assets and services later). For this example project, we will select **Business Analytics** by clicking on **Create Project**, as shown in the following screenshot:

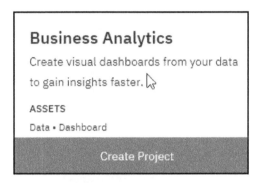

3. Next, you need to select a region from the drop-down list where your project instance will reside (I've selected **US South**):

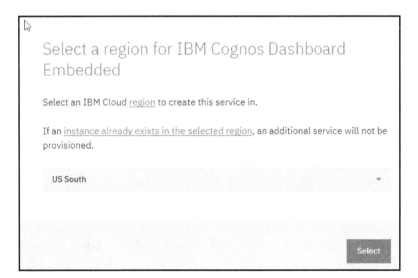

4. After clicking on **Select**, the **New project** page, which is shown in the following screenshot, allows you to provide the appropriate project details before clicking on **Create**:

Enter a name and description under **Name** and **Description.** For this example project you can leave the project, options and **Storage** and **Cognos Dashboard Embedded** information as shown in the preceding screenshot.

Once the project is created, we'll have a workspace where we can organize the assets that the project will use. There are many assets (data, collaborators, and analytic tools), but we need to start with the data. To load data into our project workspace, we can use either a direct database connector or simply drag and drop a file onto the landing zone (you can also browse to your file).

For our simple example, we are using a text file as our data source, so in the upper right of the project workspace page, you can click on the **Find and add data** icon, as shown in the following screenshot:

From there, you can click on **Load** and browse to locate and select the file that you want to use in the project (ours is `TripRuns.csv`). After the file has loaded, you then click on **Files** and you should see the file listed and ready to use:

Now that we have some data to work with, we can click on the menu selection **Add to project**, and then select **Dashboard**:

After you select **Dashboard**, you'll have to provide a name and description under **Name** and **Description**, and then click on **Save**:

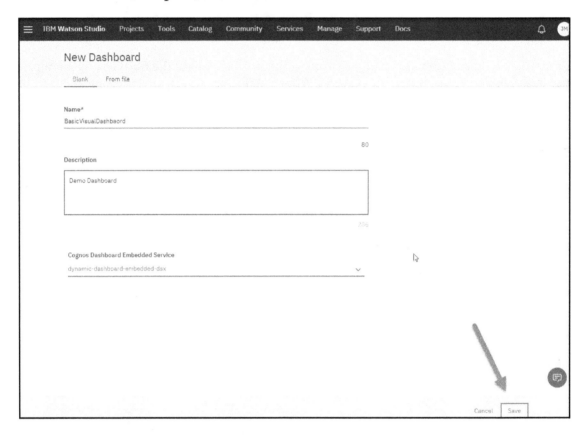

After IBM Watson sets up the new dashboard for your project, you can customize it, starting with its general layout. You can start by selecting a preformatted template:

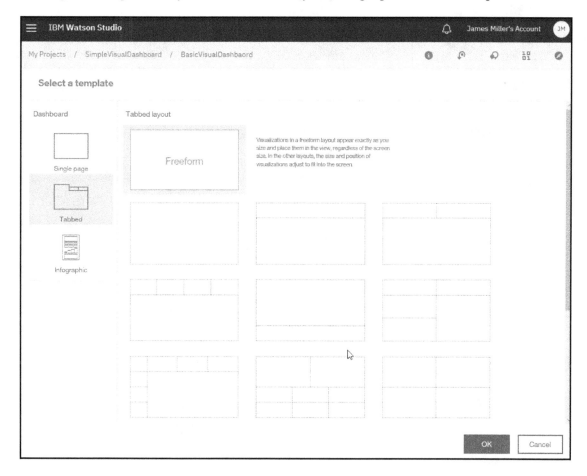

Once you select a template (I selected **Tabbed** and **Freeform**), you'll find yourself on the dashboard canvas (shown in the following screenshot), where we can design your dashboard:

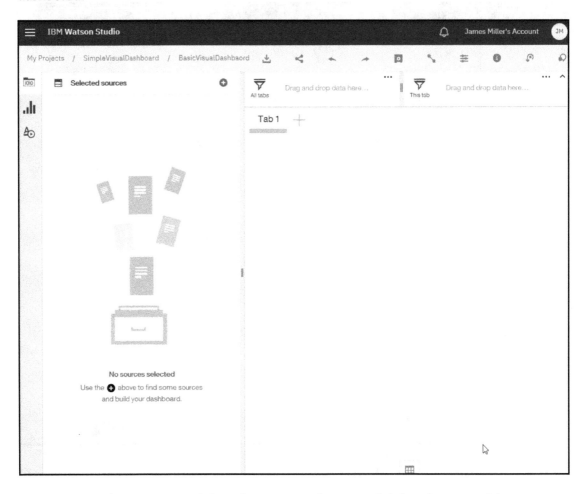

Next, click on the + icon near **Selected sources** in the upper left-hand corner of the page:

After clicking the + icon, you can then select the `TripRuns.csv` data asset that we previously added to our project:

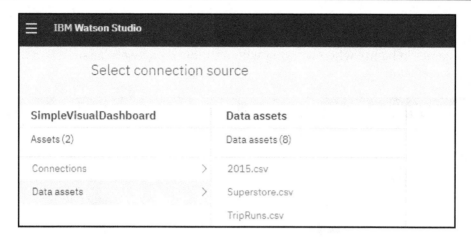

If you're wondering what **Connections** is, that is where you would define any data assets that are in the form of a direct connection to a database or other source. A **connection asset** contains the information that's required to create a connection to a data source. You create connections to IBM (or other) cloud services and on-premises databases.

After selecting our data asset, it should show up, as shown in the following screenshot. Now we are ready to proceed with constructing our dashboard:

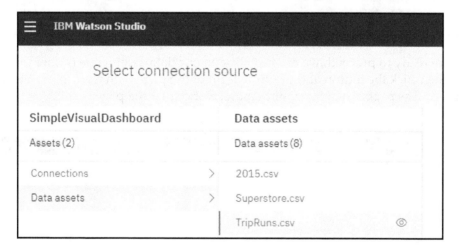

When you hover over the eye icon next to a data asset, you will notice that Watson Studio gives you the option of doing a quick review of the data asset just by clicking on the eye icon. This comes in handy when working with multiple data assets, as shown in the following screenshot:

Since we are ready to proceed, we can just click on our data asset name (rather than the eye icon) and then click the button at the bottom right of the page with the caption **Select**. The dashboard canvas page is displayed once more. Notice that the page is split into two sections, as shown in the following screenshot:

On the right is the drawing space or canvas and on the left is the menu pane, which consists of three icons: **Select sources**, **Visualizations**, and **Widgets**. We have already set up our data source, so let's click on **Visualizations**. The visualization selector is displayed, where you can select the type of visualization that you want to use on your analytics dashboard:

To keep this example simple, we just chose **Bar** as the visualization type by clicking on the **Bar** icon. A **Build your visualization** template will be added to your canvas, as shown in the following screenshot:

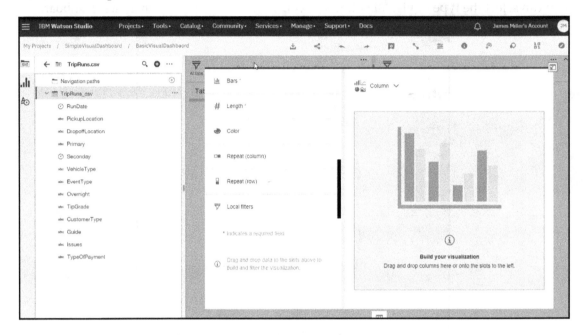

From there, we can drag and drop columns of data into the desired visualization parameters, such as **Bars** and **Length**. Note that the required parameters are denoted by a red asterisk.

As with most Watson visualization interfaces, as you add or remove the parameter values, the visualization is updated in real time:

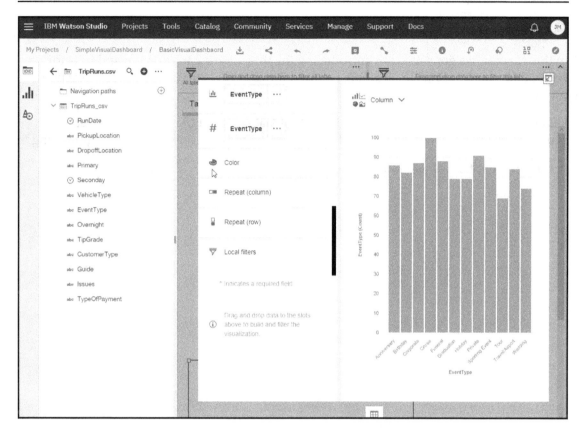

Once you are satisfied with your visualization, you can click the Save icon (located on the dashboard action bar) to save your dashboard. The dashboard that you have created is listed in the **Dashboards** section on the project's **Assets** page.

From the dashboard action bar, you are able to do the following tasks:

- Download the dashboard as a JSON file
- Create a permanent dashboard URL to share with others
- Undo/redo actions that have been performed on the dashboard
- Save the dashboard
- Add/remove widget connections
- Change dashboard properties, such as colors
- View your dashboard details, such as name and description, or choose an alternate **Cognos Dashboard Embedded** service instance if multiple services are associated with the project
- Find resources in the community, for example, useful datasets

Summary

In this chapter, we got started by introducing the IBM Cloud environment and how to access it for the first time. In addition, we used the IBM Watson console to illustrate how a project is created.

Finally, we reviewed tasks such as adding a new dataset asset to a project and creating a simple analytics dashboard with our data in minutes, without any need for programming.

In the next chapter, we will look into feature extraction.

Feature Extraction - A Bag of Tricks

2

In this chapter, we will provide a hands-on guide to the extraction and selection of features from real-life data, with emphasis on the fact that practical machine learning systems are all about proper feature engineering. This chapter will focus on teaching you the best practices for feeding data to your machine learning algorithms. Moreover, it will show you how to remove redundant data that can negatively impact the performance of your machine learning system. Lastly, it will show you some strategies for combining data from different sources.

We will cover the following topics in this chapter:

- Preprocessing
- Dimensional reduction
- Data fusion
- A bag of tricks

Preprocessing

What does preprocessing mean?

Beyond selecting a specific set of data that you want to use for a particular machine learning project, you also need to preprocess that data. This typically involves tasks such as formatting, cleaning, and sampling (or profiling). We won't be delving too far into the definitions of each of these tasks, and will assume that the reader grasps their meaning and purpose. We'll say that **formatting** is a way of simply putting the data source into a form that can be easily understood and consumed within your project. **Cleaning** is mostly concerned with removing unwanted data and **sampling** is all about reducing the overall size of the data for performance reasons.

Although, being a developer at heart, I am anxious to take on these tasks by crafting a script or perusing and selecting a function from an open source library, instead, let's explore what Watson Studio offers us for achieving these objectives.

The data refinery

As part of preprocessing, Watson Studio gives you the ability to refine data. Refining data is described in the online documentation as the cleansing and shaping of data.

As you manipulate data within Watson Studio using the refinery feature, you build what is referred to as a customized data refinery flow. We can try out some of the features and functions offered by the data refinery by going through the following steps (starting with some setup):

1. To create a project, you click on **New project** on the right side of the Watson Studio **My Projects** page, as shown in the following screenshot:

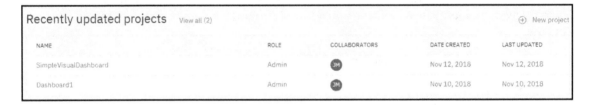

2. Next, choose a project starter. We'll choose **Data Engineering**, as shown in the following screenshot (you may need to select or provision the required services at this step, depending upon what you selected; for our selection, no additional services are needed):

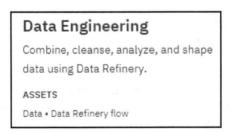

3. On the **New project** screen, you can add a name and description for the project, as shown in the following screenshot:

At this point, you need to choose whether to restrict who you can add as collaborators (we'll use the default settings in this example), and you might be prompted to add services as you add assets that require them (in this example, no additional services will be needed, but as an FYI, you can also add other services after you create a project using the **Settings** page).

4. Next, click on **Create**, as shown in the following screenshot:

After clicking on **Create**, Watson Studio will prepare the project for you, displaying the dialog shown in the following screenshot:

And finally (typically, it only takes a minute or two), your new project will open, ready to go, and you can start having fun developing it!

Data

Of course, every project needs data, and so the next step is to add data to our project. When you add data, it is considered a **data asset**, and by default, all of the project's collaborators are automatically authorized to access the data. Go through the following steps to add a data file to your project:

1. From the project's **Assets** page, click on the Find and add data icon, as shown in the following screenshot:

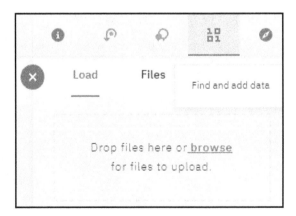

2. Next, click on **Load** and then browse to find the file or drag it onto the **Load** pane, as shown in the following screenshot:

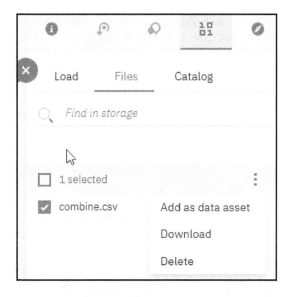

 You must stay on the page until the load is complete. You can cancel an ongoing load process if you want to stop loading a file. Be advised that there really isn't any progress indicator while the file is loading, so give it a few minutes!!

The file we are using in this project (combine.csv) is a comma-delimited text file containing statistics on players who attended the NFL scouting combine.

3. The files you add are saved in the object storage bin that is associated with your project and are listed as data assets on the **Assets** page of your project (as you can see in the preceding screenshot). From there, you must select the specific file and click on **Add as data asset**. At that point, you will be prompted to click on **Apply**, as shown in the following screenshot:

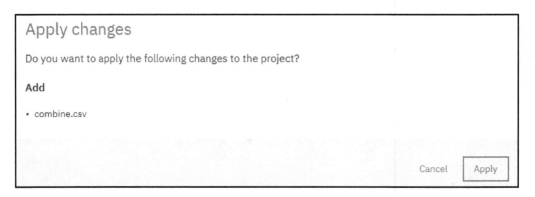

Now, we are ready to use the file in our project:

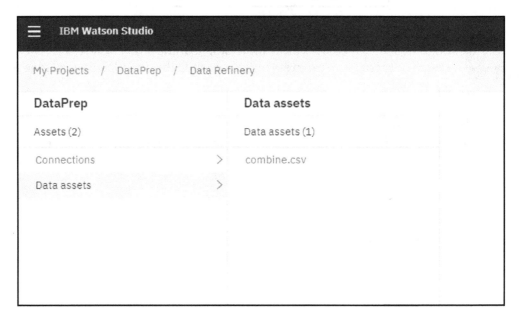

Adding the refinery

Let's go through the following steps to add the refinery:

1. To access the IBM Watson Studio data refinery, you can click on **Add to project**, as shown in the following screenshot:

2. Then, choose **Data Refinery Flow**, as shown in the following screenshot:

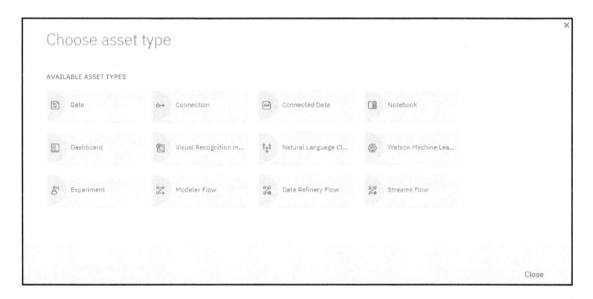

3. After you've invoked the refinery, you need to add our data file (by clicking on the data asset (file)) and then click on **Add** at the bottom-right of the page. Once the data is read into the refinery (as shown in the following screenshot), you will be ready to process it:

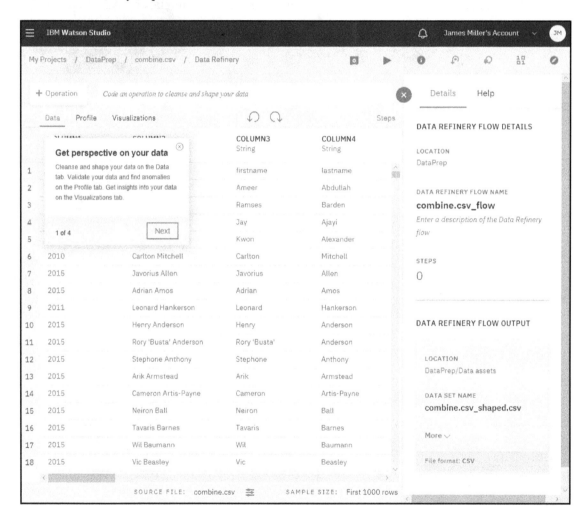

Refining data by using commands

Rather than using scripting to process or refine your data, you can use commands (also known as **operations**) to preprocess the data. To do this, you can start by entering a command (or **operation name**) and let Watson Studio's autocomplete function help you find the right operation and syntax (no programming involved!).

> Note that, if you hover over any operation or function name, you'll see both a description and detailed information for completing the command.

When you're ready, you can then click on **Apply** to add the operation to your data refinery flow.

For example, you might want to sort or reorder a column of data. If you start typing arra, you'll see the following result:

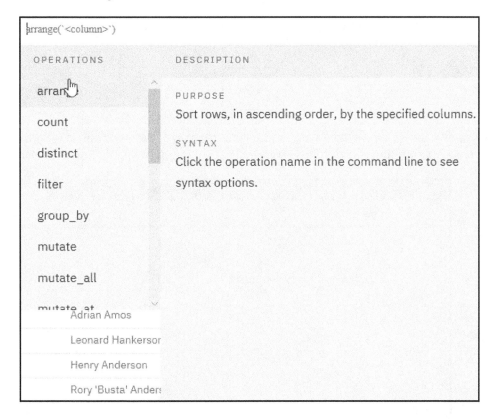

If you then click to select the **arrange()** function, you can click on the **()** and select a column from your data file, as shown in the following screenshot:

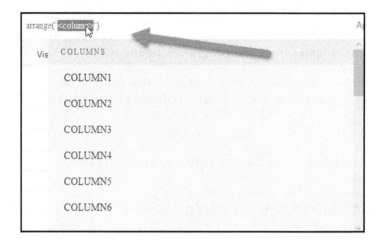

When you're ready, click on the **Apply** button to add the command to the data refinery flow, as shown in the following screenshot:

Without saving the data refinery (more on this in a moment), Watson Studio will display the effect of applying the command to your data, as shown in the following screenshot:

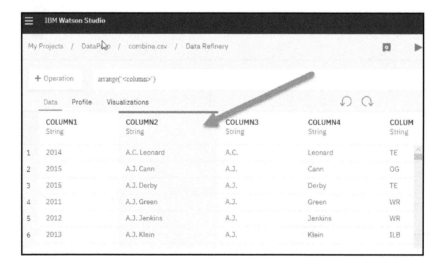

There are numerous commands available to add to the data refinery flow. Each command will be added as a step within the flow. If you click on **Steps** (as shown in the following screenshot) you can view and edit each of the steps you have defined for the flow; you can even delete them, if you wish. In our case, I have added three steps: the first to arrange (sort) the data, the second to convert the first column from a string into an integer, and the third to filter out only those records for the years before 2011, as shown in the following screenshot:

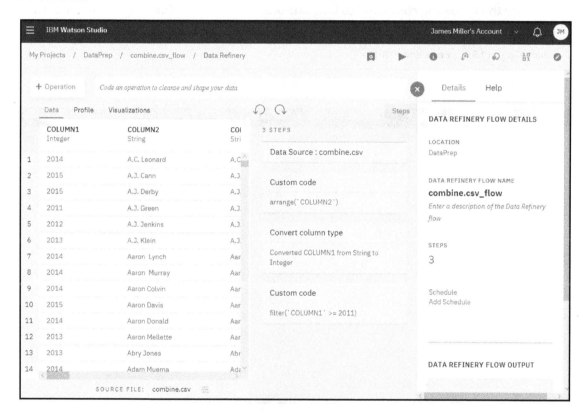

At any time, you can save and run the data refinery flow by clicking the save data refinery flow and run data refinery flow icons shown in the following screenshot:

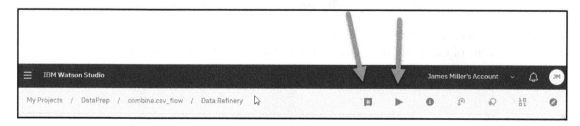

Again, there are commands to perform almost any of the preprocessing tasks required in most machine learning projects, such as `group`, `rename`, `sample_n`, and `summarize`. Perhaps most importantly, the data refinery provides scripting support for the many `dplyr` R library operations, functions, and logical operators. For example, `sample_frac` and `sample_n` are supported by the data refinery and are very useful for generating sample datasets for your original data source.

We can use the following command to take our original file (`combine_.csv`) and create a data refinery flow to generate a sample:

```
Sample_n(199, replace=TRUE)
```

The preceding command will generate the following output:

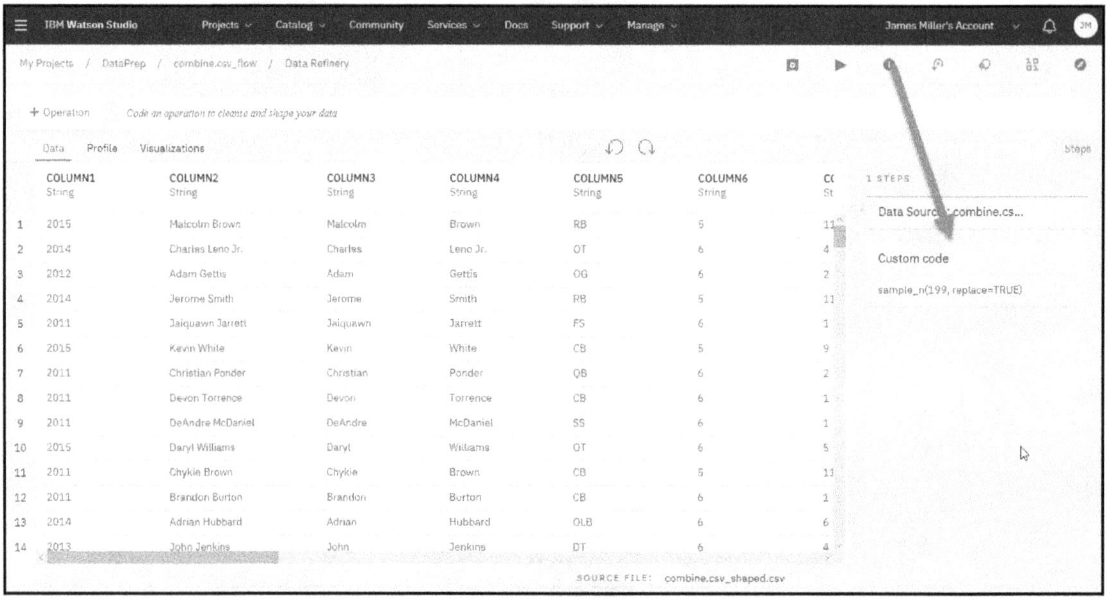

This will automatically read our original file and create a a random sample of data based on the number of rows indicated (in our case, 99). The `replace` parameter indicates that if a dataset already exists with the output filename, then it will be overwritten.

After saving and running the data refinery flow, we will see a summary of our results (along with a list of our prior runs), as shown in the following screenshot:

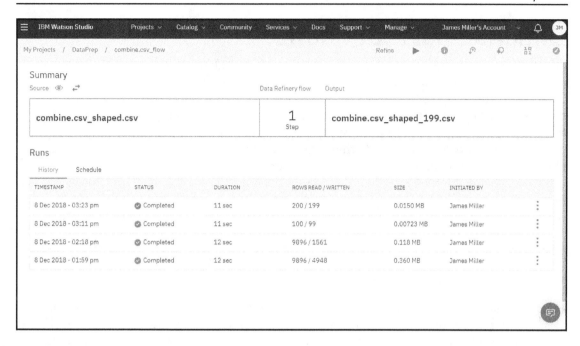

We can see that we have created a sample file from the original, named `combine.csv_sharped_199.csv`, as shown in the following screenshot:

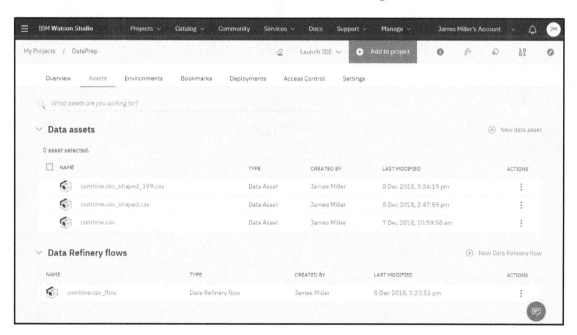

Dimensional reduction

Dimensional reduction is usually used to reduce the number of variables that are to be considered in an machine learning project. It is often used where columns of data in a file have more than an acceptable number of missing values, have low variance, or are extremely variable in nature. Before attempting to reduce your data source by removing those unwanted columns, you need to be comfortable that this is the right thing to be doing. In other words, you want to make sure that the data you reduce does not create a bias in the remaining data. Profiling the data is an excellent way to determine whether the dimensional reduction of a particular column or columns is appropriate. **Data profiling** is a technique that is used to examine **data** to determine its accuracy and completeness. This is the process of examining a **data source** to uncover the erroneous sections in the **data**.

You can create effective scripts to accomplish this, and, as expected, there are numerous packages and libraries available to for you to download and use. However, once again, Watson Studio can easily do this for us.

We can gather the information we need to profile our data source without the need for scripting or programming by creating a data asset profile. The profile of a data asset created by Watson Studio by default includes generated metadata and statistics about the textual content of a data file.

To create a profile for your data, you can go to the asset's **Profile** page and click on **Create Profile**.

 You can update any existing profile when the data changes.

After clicking on **Create Profile**, the results will be displayed, as shown in the following screenshot:

You can take a minute or two to scroll though the generated profile to view the various statistics, such as the overall number of columns and rows. You can search by column or data point, value frequencies, unique values, min/max, mean, and so on.

Data fusion

Data fusion is not a data analysis practice, but rather describes the integration of data from disparate sources. Thankfully, you will find that you can use Watson Studio to collect and combine data sources without much effort.

With Watson Studio, you can set up a **catalog** for all of your data sources so that you can easily find and share data (and other assets). A catalog is a defined private space within an environment or organization. It is a way to organize your resources across many data science projects—resources such as data assets and analytical assets—and can be used to manage the access that users have to each of these assets.

What is particularly exciting about this feature is the fact that you can organize and control access to many different types of asset within a single catalog including the following:

- Data in files
- Connected data
- Connections themselves
- Folders
- A host of other analytical assets (which we'll experiment with later in this book)

Catalog setup

Creating a catalog is easy. Let's create a catalog by going through the following steps:

1. Start by clicking on **Catalog**, then **View All Catalogs**, and then **New Catalog**, as shown in the following screenshot:

2. Then provide, some basic information, such as a name and a description for your new catalog, and then click on **Create**, as shown in the following screenshot:

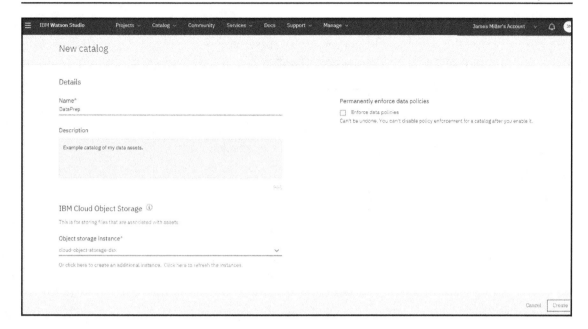

Almost instantly, the fresh new catalog will be created and ready to be used, as shown in the following screenshot:

3. To add some assets to the catalog, you can click on **Add to Catalog** (in the top-right of the page) and select the type of asset you want to add (**Local files**, **Connected asset**, or **Connection**), as shown in the following screenshot:

4. Here, we will just add some local files to our catalog. Once we click on **Local files**, the **Add data assets from local files** page will be displayed (as shown in the follow screenshot), where you can browse and select the files you want to add:

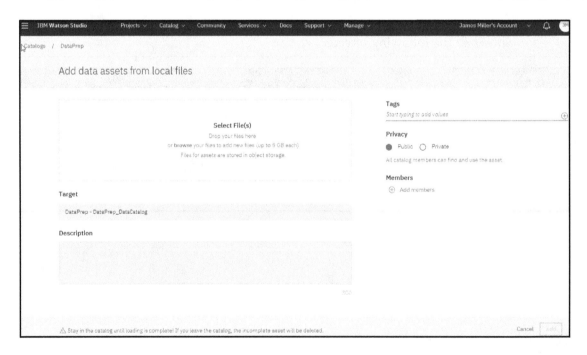

5. Once you have added all of your files to this page, you must click on **Add**, as shown in the following screenshot:

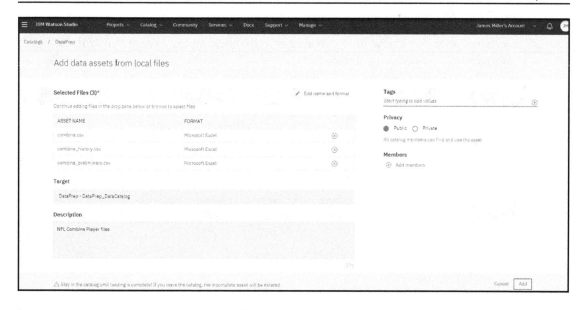

Again, after a short pause, the catalog will be updated, organized, and ready to use, as shown in the following screenshot:

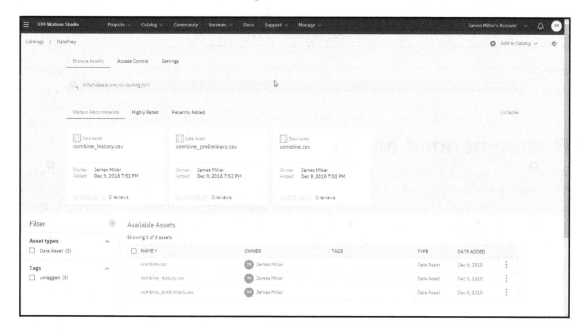

6. Once you create and update your catalog, you can mange who can access the catalog, as well as how they can access it, by clicking on **Access Control**, as shown in the following screenshot:

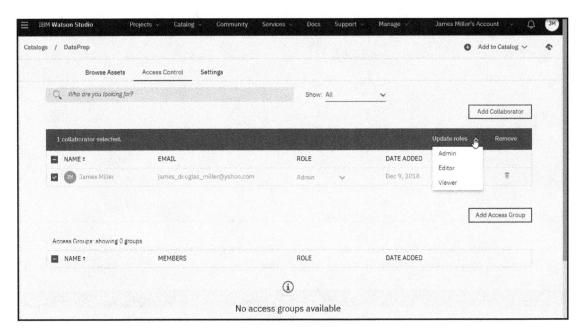

Watson Studio catalogs allow collaborators to quickly and easily find, preview, rate, and consume each asset in the catalog. We will look at catalogs in more detail later in this book.

Recommended assets

Another cool feature of Watson Studio catalogs is that Watson Studio actually uses **Watson Machine Learning** to derive a list of assets that you haven't accessed yet based on attributes common to the assets that you've viewed, created, and added to projects, such as tags, asset classification, attribute classifiers, data types, asset owners, and asset types. The more assets you access and catalog, the better the recommendations are. Again, we'll dig deeper into this feature in later chapters of this book!

A bag of tricks

The more orderly you are in your handling of data, the more consistent and better results you are like likely to achieve (with any project). The process for getting data ready for a machine learning algorithm (selecting, preprocessing, and transforming) can be accomplished using IBM Watson Studio with little programming or scripting required and, by leveraging the data refinery and catalog features, the work that you did at the start can be used over and over with little or no reworking required.

Here are a few parting words of advice:

- Take the time to add descriptions for your assets and always use descriptive names
- Manage your data assets well: remove extraneous copies or test versions right away and keep your catalogs clean
- Use the profiling feature religiously to better understand your assets
- Control who can access your assets by managing project and asset collaborators

Summary

In this chapter, we jumped right into using IBM Watson Studio's various features to accomplish various data preprocessing and setup objectives, such as using built-in R libraries for data preprocessing, dimensional reduction, and data fusion. We then offered a number of recommendations to save you time when preparing an ML project.

In the next chapter, we'll examine the machine learning paradigm and focus on various approaches and algorithms. The chapter will start by giving a practical background to model evaluation, model selection, and algorithm selection in machine learning and will then cover supervised learning.

3
Supervised Machine Learning Models for Your Data

This chapter (along with previous two) acts as the backbone for the entire book. It provides a tour of the machine learning paradigm—the features and functionalities available through the IBM Cloud and IBM Watson platforms, with a focus on well-known approaches and algorithms. We'll start the chapter by giving a somewhat practical background to what model evaluation, model selection, and algorithm selection in machine learning entail. Next, we will look at how the IBM Cloud platform can help to simplify and fast-track the entire process.

Moreover, this chapter will discuss machine learning algorithms for classification and regression problems, and again approach these topics using the IBM Cloud platform. By the end of the chapter, the reader should be able to not only understand the concepts involved in selecting an appropriate classification technique and estimators, but be able to build and deploy basic machine learning models for the data at hand, using IBM Cloud.

We'll divide this chapter into the following areas:

- Model selection
- Testing the model
- Classification
- Regression
- Testing the predictive capability

Model selection

Machine learning has become more and more ordinary, and understanding which machine learning algorithm (or model type) to use, based upon your data and objectives, is important, and if you are relatively new to the process, it can be daunting.
Fitting a model to training data is one thing, but how do you know that the model (technique) or algorithm you select will generalize well to all your data and create the best prediction? Too much training or overfitting doesn't solve this problem; in fact, in this situation, it is typical for the model to perform poorly with totally new data.

Once again, the IBM Cloud platform provides robust and practical tools to assist you with this process.

The cloud offers a machine learning service (IBM Watson Machine Learning). The service offers the ability to manage your developed machine learning models using a continuous learning system, as well as an easy method for deployment, including online, batch, and streaming modes.

 You can head over to the following link to know more about IBM Watson Machine Learning: `https://console.bluemix.net/catalog/services/machine-learning`.

In addition, the model builder offered in IBM Watson Studio (which includes tutorials and sample datasets to illustrate how to train different types of machine learning models without the need for coding) can get you going quickly by stepping you through the, perhaps tedious, task of model selection (and even evaluation and deployment).

 Later in this chapter, we will refer to a provided data asset to illustrate the process of bringing the reader to an understanding of the process of selecting a model type, steps to train the model and evaluating the models performance.

IBM Watson Studio Model Builder

The Model Builder in IBM Watson Studio is a graphical tool that actually guides you, step by step, through building your first machine learning models. The model builder utilizes the following workflow:

1. Upload data to train
2. Choose a machine learning technique and algorithm
3. Train and evaluate the model
4. Test and deploy the model

The model builder (currently) focuses on creating three basic types of machine learning model techniques (which is typically more than sufficient for starting out with most machine learning projects). Furthermore, for each kind of model, you can choose from multiple algorithms to implement within the model. These are referred to as model techniques.

Part of the angst of building a machine learning solution is selecting the proper ML algorithm to be used. If unsure, or in the interest of saving time, at least for your first few attempts, you may want to utilize the option of having the model builder automatically select an algorithm for you, based upon the training data you provide. The model techniques include the following:

- **Binary classifier**: Classifies data into two categories
- **Multiclass classifier**: Classifies data into multiple categories
- **Regression**: Predicts a value from a continuous set of values

Using the model builder

Let's now step through some initial illustrations of using the model builder:

1. To use the model builder, you need to add the Watson Machine Learning service as an asset to a new or existing project (this is referred to as associating the service with the project). To do this from within your project, you can click on **Add to project** and then choose the **WATSON MACHINE LEARNING** service as the asset type, as shown in the following screenshot:

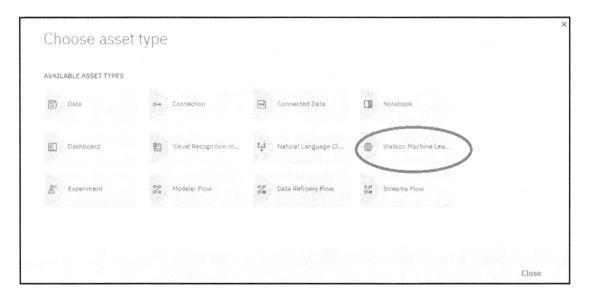

2. Once you have added this service to your project, you can then create and add new models to the project simply by clicking on **New Watson Machine Learning model** under **Models**:

3. On the **New model** page (as shown in the following screenshot), you must provide your new model's basic details as follows:

- **Name**: The name of your new model.
- **Description**: A description of your model.
- **Machine Learning Service**: The service that the model will use (there are others, but for now, we'll select the IBM Watson Machine Learning service: **Machine Learning-bg**).
- **Select model type**: In this first attempt, we want to have **Model builder** help us choose the model type and algorithms, so you can select **Automatic**.
- **Select runtime**: Select the runtime environment (just use the **Default Spark Scala 2.11** option for now). Runtime environments are the combination of memory, space and CPUs which can effect pricing and cost. You can review the details of various runtimes online (`https://dataplatform.cloud.ibm.com/docs/content/wsj/console/environment-runtimes.html`).

4. Finally, you can click on **Create**:

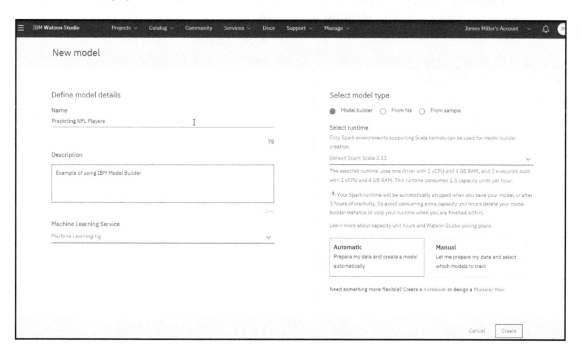

Scala has gained a lot of popularity and is widely used by large number of companies. Scala and Spark are being used at Facebook, Pinterest, Netflix, Conviva, and TripAdvisor for big data and machine learning applications. The IBM Cloud platform offers Scala as one of its defaults.

If you miss or skip the step of associating a machine learning service, when you click on **Create,** you will see the following message:

Machine Learning Service

No Machine Learning service instances associated with your project.

Associate a Machine Learning service instance with your project on the project settings page, then click the reload button below to refresh the instances available for association with your new model builder instance.

Reload

5. If you do see this message, you will need to click the **Associate a Machine Learning service instance** link, select a service, and then click on **Reload** before you can proceed with creating the model.

Training data

At this point, we need to select some training data for our model. So, from the **Select data asset** page, we need to locate our specific data asset (file), click on the selection radio button to the left of it, and click on **Next**:

As a note, the **Select data asset** page makes it easy to determine which data asset to use for training the model with features such as **Click to preview data**:

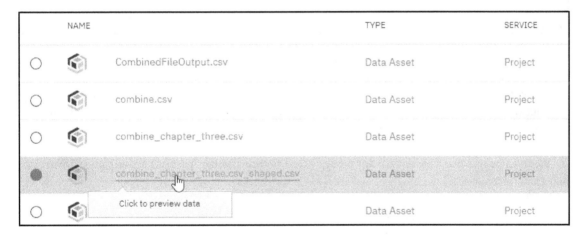

By hovering over any listed asset and then clicking on it(Click to preview date), Watson will retrieve and load the data for you to review.

You cannot alter or refine data here, but you can scroll through it to make sure that this is the data asset that you want to use to train your model. If you are satisfied that you want to use this data in your model, you can click on **Use This Data**:

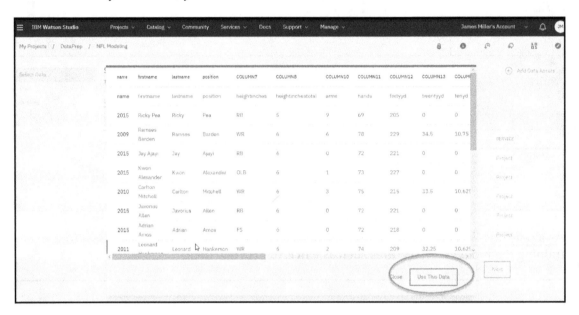

At this point, it is time to select one of the three model techniques to use. First, you choose what you want to predict (the column in your data file, known as the label column, for which you want the model to predict its value) and the columns to use to determine the prediction. These are known as the columns of data in the data asset that the model should feature—or the feature columns.

You can then use the model builder's suggested technique (or in other words algorithm) or select your own:

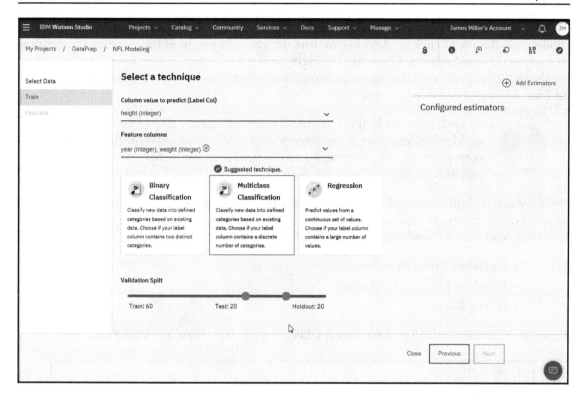

One of the clear advantages of using the model builder is that you can easily try before you buy, so to speak. In other words, if you are not sure as to which modeling technique to select and use, you have the opportunity to use and evaluate each option quickly and with minimal investment. In the preceding example, I elected to use a very simple tryst: I want the model to predict a player's height, given his weight, for a selected year (or NFL season).

Looking at the model technique options offered, **Multiclass Classification** is the process of classifying instances into one of three or more classes; **Binary Classification**; is the classification of instances into one of the two classes, and **Regression** would work with a large number of classes.

Guessing which technique to use

In this example, the values for height would most likely have more than two possible values, and hence we might choose **Multiclass Classification** or even **Regression**. Again, it would be best, since the model builder makes quick work of this, to try both and then evaluate the results.

Moving on, if you indicated a manual approach (or selected the **Manual** mode) to build the model, you'll have to click on **Add Estimators** (in the upper right of the page) to choose one or more specific estimators. Choosing the right model estimator is often even harder than choosing the technique. Different estimators are a better match for different types of data and for solving different problems.

 As we'll see later in this chapter, the model builder allows you to select multiple estimators for the same model and train on each of them so that you can then easily compare and contrast each estimator's performance results together on the same page.

With the model builder, based upon the classification technique chosen, you'll have a number of estimators to choose from (as shown in the following screenshot). For example, we chose **Multiclass Classification**, so you could pick one of the following estimators:

- **Decision Tree Classifier**
- **Random Forecast Classifier**
- **Naive Bayes**

Here, we will choose the **Random Forest Classifier** estimator and click on **Add**:

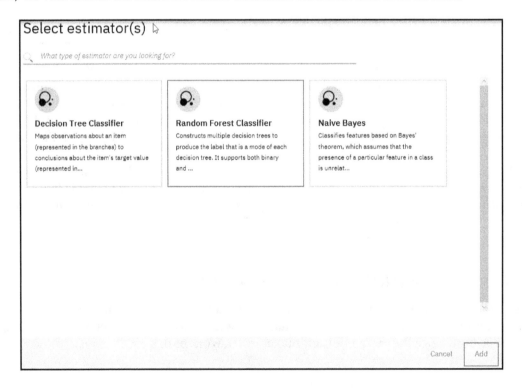

After clicking **Add**, and then **Next**, the model will be trained on the data, technique, and estimator selected. The results will then be posted to the **Select model** page (as shown in the following screenshot), where you can click on **Save** to save the model results for evaluation:

A Watson Machine Learning model (created with the Model Builder) becomes an asset and is listed as such (shown above) on the IBM Watson Studio project page for later reference, refinement and reuse.

It is worth mentioning that an approach to learning how to select a classification technique (algorithm) and estimator is through experimentation with the model builder. In other words, using the broader terms of classification and feature selection, the model builder now makes it effective and efficient enough to test hypotheses with a variety of approaches, easily assess the results, and then deploy the best fit (more on evaluating model performance and accuracy in a later section of this chapter and throughout this book) as a continuous learning model with new and unseen data.

We will see more on this process with some experimentation later in this chapter.

Deployment

Deployment of a predictive model so that it can be leveraged in routine decision-making is typically a somewhat complex process due to a variety of challenges, and let's face it—predictive models that never get deployed never add value.

When you create a model by using the IBM Watson Studio model builder, you can deploy the model directly from the model builder after you train it. Even better, after you deploy your model, you can set up a continuous learning and evaluation process for your model.

When you deploy a model, you save it to the model repository that is associated with your Watson Machine Learning service, where you can then use your deployed model to score data and build an application.

Model builder deployment steps

To deploy our predictive model, we can use the following steps:

1. On the model page, click on **Add Deployment**.
2. On the **Deploy model** page, select the **Online** deployment type and enter a deployment name and description.
3. Click on **Deploy**.
4. When model deployment is complete, from the **ACTIONS** menu (circled in the following screenshot), click on **View**:

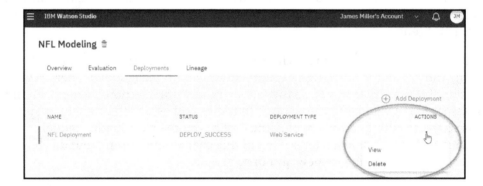

The deployment details window appears, showing three tabs: **Overview**, **Implementation**, and **Test** (as shown in the following screenshot):

Testing the model

Now is a good time to have a look at how you can test the model prediction right here in IBM Watson Studio. To do this, you can click on **Test**:

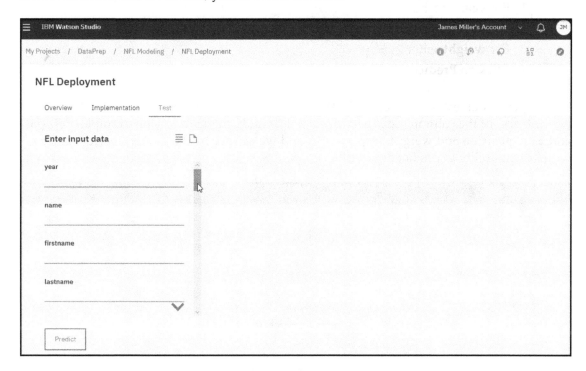

The default test format generated shows you an input form that you can use to enter data values. Later, you'll see that if you have an external process generating test data, you can use the input format icons to use JSON data file format and paste in your data test values:

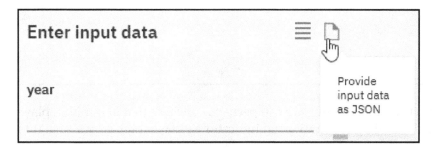

For now (staying on the **Test** tab), leave the default format (input form) and enter some values for the important columns (the input data form is populated with a sample record from the dataset). To test the model, change the values and click on **Predict**:

1. For **year**, enter 2016
2. For **position**, enter QB
3. For **weight**, enter 225
4. Click on **Predict**

Once your model test is complete, IBM Watson Studio displays a graphical score (with percentages) of the column's ability to predict the result. In the following example, fields **5** and **6** are **position** and **weight**, respectively, and we can see by the model's performance scores, their ability to predict the result:

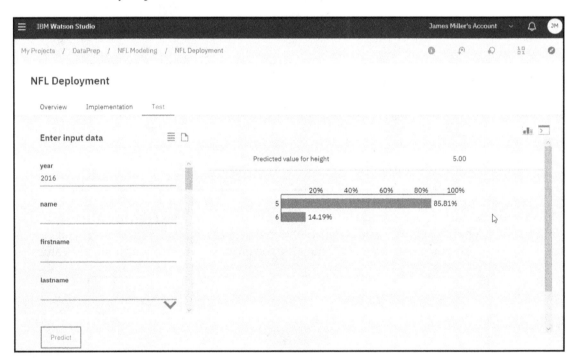

So, given the preceding output, we can perhaps conclude that in our NFL player statistical file, a player's position is a pretty good indicator as to what the player's height is.

If you are so inclined, you can click the output formatting icon (shown circled in the following screenshot) and convert the performance information to raw output (**View raw output**):

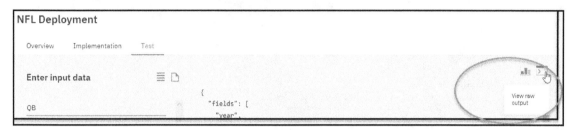

When you deploy your model in this way (using Watson Studio deploy), the deployment is a one-time event. In other words, you enter your data, train the model on the data, then see the performance results and draw your conclusions.

This works for exploration and investigation purposes, but realistically, you'd want to retain and continually train the model with new data as it becomes available. To do this, you can use the IBM Watson Machine Learning continuous learning system, which provides automated monitoring of model performance (discussed briefly in the next section of this chapter), retraining, and redeployment to ensure prediction quality from your model.

Continuous learning and model evaluation

Although we won't take the time to go deeply into this topic here in this chapter, IBM Watson Studio does provide a straightforward method to accomplish this, using a model you developed and deployed using the model builder. This method does require choosing a **Spark Service or Environment** option and establishing a feedback data store as a project resource, which is where the resulting model performance metrics will be retained (saved).

These resources can be configured using the **Configure performance monitoring** page shown in the following screenshot:

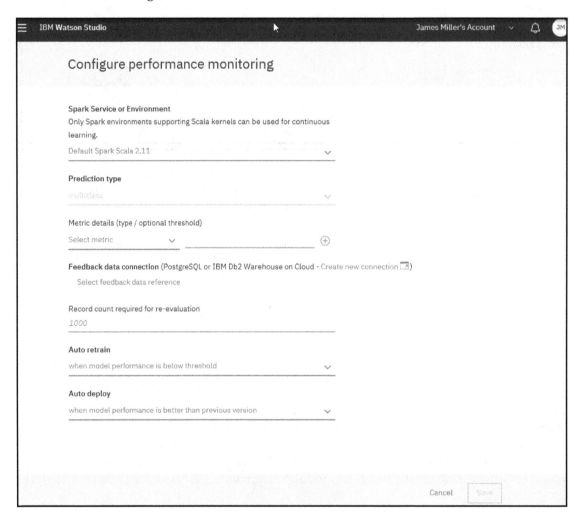

Once you establish a (feedback) data store, you can use Watson Studio and the model builder to easily define metrics and triggers as part of a continuous learning process and periodically review the updated model performance metrics and use chart controls to switch metrics or to view the results as a chart or as a table.

Classification

Classification is a key concept in both machine learning and statistics. We've shown that the model builder offers both binary and multiclass classification techniques (as well as regression). Earlier in this chapter, we used the model builder and arbitrarily selected a classification technique just to show how easy it is to build, train, and deploy a model using the tool. In this section, we will take a closer look at each technique and which choice would make the most sense, given our training data.

Binary classification

Binary (also referred to as **binomial**) classification is the process of classifying the elements of a given set into two groups on the basis of a classification rule. The product documentation offers a great example exercise that you can use to understand when binary classification is perhaps the best choice for your model. The example is training a model to predict whether or not a customer is likely to buy a tent from an outdoor equipment store, given the training data sample. If you go ahead and download the sample data and then examine the columns, you can understand how binary classification works. Let's analyze the exercise.

We want to build a model that will predict whether a given customer is likely to purchase a particular product; in this case, a tent. Suppose we again use the model builder to create a new model, load the sample data provided, and set the basic model details.

The process is as follows:

1. Define a label column. In this example, the choice is IS_TENT. This column indicates whether or not the customer bought a tent.
2. Define the feature columns. Feature columns are columns in the data that contain the traits on which the machine learning model will base its predictions. In this historical data, there are the following four feature columns:

   - GENDER: Customer gender
   - AGE: Customer age
   - MARITAL_STATUS: Married, Single, or Unspecified
   - PROFESSION: General category of the customer's profession, such as **Hospitality** or **Sales**, or simply **Other**

3. Set the build type to **Automatic** (this will cause model builder to automatically select an algorithm to implement the machine learning technique you specify).
4. Click on **Create** and add the training data.

To train the model, you will specify the preceding label and feature columns and then pick the machine learning technique: binary classification. After the model is saved, the model details page will open automatically. To see which algorithm the model builder used, you can go to the **Summary** table in the **Overview** information on the model details page (shown in the following screenshot) and click on **View** in the **Model builder details** row:

This will reveal the following details for review:

ℹ️ Model Builder Details

Input data set	GoSales.csv
Problem type	binary
Training / validation data split	Train: 60%, Test: 20%, Holdout: 20%
Transformers	Auto Data Preparation
Selected estimator	LogisticRegression
Other trained estimators	

Close

You can see that the model builder, after we picked binary classification, chose **LogisticRegression** as its best choice for an estimator. Logistic regression is the usual choice when the dependent variable is dichotomous (binary). In our case, the dependent variable is our label column, IS_TENT.

The conclusion, considering our data and objective, is that binary classification was picked as the technique because we want to classify the data into defined categories (think about how the records in the training data could be grouped, for example: males, married, who work in sales; males, single, who work as a professional; and so on). The estimator used (logistic regression) was chosen since, again, the dependent variable is binary (will purchase or will not purchase).

Aligning the sample data values with the chosen technique and estimator, the reasoning behind these choices should begin to make sense. It is a good idea to continue to experiment with data and the model builder to gain further comfort with these concepts.

Multiclass classification

Multiclass (also referred to as **multinomial**) classification is the duty of classifying elements of a prearranged set into one of three or more groups. Again, the product documentation provides a good example of this: training a model to predict which product category is most likely to interest a customer in an outdoor equipment store.

In the previous section, the example used the same data, but this example use case is looking to determine a product category (group) as the result, rather than a particular purchase decision. The model built in this example will predict which product line is most likely to interest a given customer.

Stepping through the example process, we'll have the same training data and the same feature columns (as the prior example) but a different label column: PRODUCT_LINE. Also, in this example, rather than picking **Automatic**, choose **Manual** so that you can choose the specific algorithms the model uses.

So, to train this model, you will specify the preceding label and feature columns and then pick the machine learning technique: **Multiclass Classification**. Another difference in this exercise is that we want to add two estimators (algorithm choices) for the model to use so that we can compare each performance:

1. Click **Add Estimators** to view the estimators (algorithms) that are available to use with the multiclass classification technique in the model builder.
2. Click the card labeled **Naive Bayes** and then click on **Add**.
3. Click on **Add Estimators** again.
4. Click the card labeled **Random Forest Classifier** and then click on **Add**:

A neat feature with the model builder is that, after the training completes, you can see evaluations of both algorithm choices (as seen in the following screenshot):

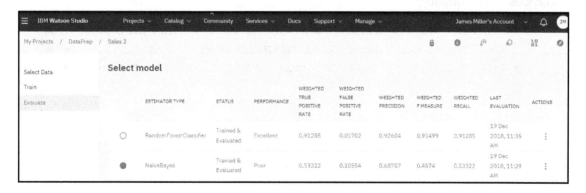

In the preceding screenshot, you can see that the performance evaluation of the model using **Naive Bayes** is rated as **Poor**, while the performance of the model using random forest classification is **Excellent**. Consider the following, as I have mentioned already in this chapter, and as is even stated in the product documentation.

> *"To find the best solution for a given machine learning problem, you sometimes have to experiment with your training data, the model design, and/or the algorithms used. With the model builder, you can easily compare the results of different algorithms used (to better understand what the best choice should be)."*

This is extremely good and practical advice, especially to those relatively new to machine learning.

Let's now move on to the final topic of this chapter: regression.

Regression

Regression is essentially a statistical approach used to find the relationship between variables. In machine learning, this is used to predict the outcome of an event based on the relationship between variables obtained from the dataset.

As we've seen with prior options for training a model, the product documentation gives us a very good example exercise we can use to illustrate the regression approach to machine learning: training a model to predict the amount of money a customer is likely to spend on a trip to an outdoor equipment store.

Again, we'll go over the appropriate steps required for this exercise. For this exercise, we will choose the following:

- PURCHASE_AMOUNT (which is the average amount of money the customer has spent on each visit to the store) as our label column
- GENDER, AGE, MARITAL_STATUS, and PROFESSION as our feature columns

Next, as in the preceding section's exercise, we will again click on **Manual** so that we will be able to choose the specific algorithms the model uses (instead of letting the model builder chose for us), then perform the following steps:

1. For the **Select a technique** option (shown in the following screenshot), select **Regression**.
2. Add the estimator named **Gradient Boosted Tree Regressor**. The following screenshot indicates the parameters we've chosen for this exercise model build:

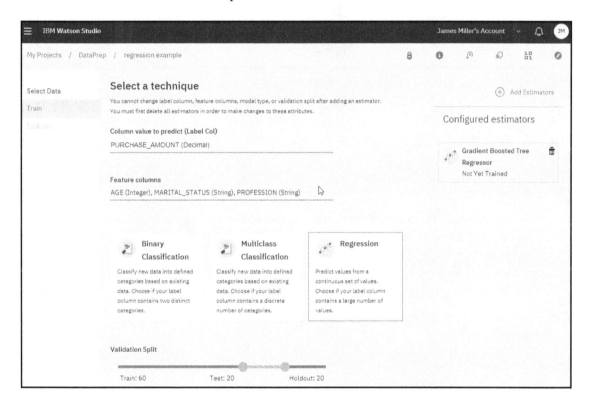

3. Once the preceding details are set, you can click on **Next** to begin training the model with the sample data, using the selected technique and estimator. After training completes, you can click on **Save**. Of course, after the model is saved, the model details page opens automatically:

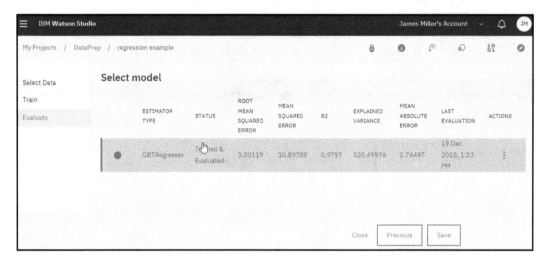

4. In the usual fashion, to verify the algorithm the model builder used, you can again go to the **Summary** table in the **Overview** information on the model details page (shown in the following screenshot) and click on **View** in the **Model builder details** row:

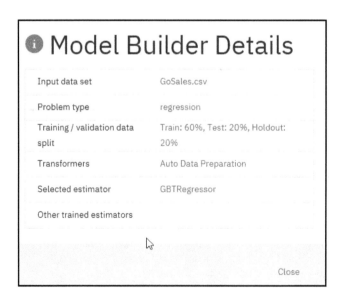

Testing the predictive capability

Another useful feature of the model builder is that it provides you with the ability to easily test the predictive ability of a deployed model, without having to do any programming.

To test a deployed model from the deployment details page, perform the following steps:

1. First, in the **Test** area of the deployment details page, there will be a simple input form (see the following screenshot), where you can type in some values for the feature columns: GENDER, AGE, MARITAL_STATUS, and PROFESSION (you can ignore the other fields in the form):

2. Next, click on **Predict** to create a prediction based upon the values that you just entered and the model you have built. This will be the prediction of how much money a customer with the entered attributes is likely to spend on a trip to the store. The following screenshot shows the result of a test. The predicted amount of spend is $118.81:

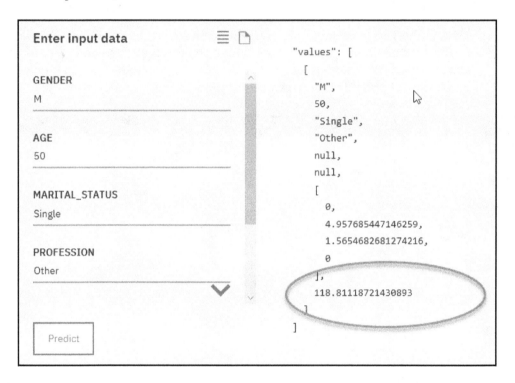

As the documentation suggests, you can take additional value combinations from the training file and enter them into the input data form to do additional testing.

Summary

In this chapter, we discussed the significance of model selection; specifically, selecting classification techniques and related estimators. We saw how using the IBM Cloud platform and Watson Studio offers a way to explore the performance of various techniques and estimators in an efficient and effective way. Using this easy exploration process, you can feel confident that your selected model fits to the data well. We also saw how to use Watson Studio to build, deploy, and test a model and configure it for continuous learning.

In the next chapter, we will discuss the difference between supervised and unsupervised learning, as well as looking at semi-supervised learning. Moreover, we will look at the concept of clustering algorithms, and examine online versus batch learning.

4
Implementing Unsupervised Algorithms

In `Chapter 3`, *Supervised Machine Learning Models for Your Data*, we focused on *supervised* machine learning algorithms. This chapter will build on the previous chapters in that we will continue the tour of the machine learning paradigm offered in IBM Cloud. The chapter will cover **supervised** versus **unsupervised** as well as **semi-supervised** learning.

Supervised learning problems are usually categorized into **regression** and **classification** problems, and we saw the ways that using IBM Watson Studio and its model builder feature can help solve for those sort of problems.

Unsupervised learning, on the other hand, allows us to approach problems when we might have little or no idea what the results should or would look like. Here, in these types of problems, we can attempt to derive structure from the data itself by **clustering** (the data) based upon relationships identified among the variables within the data, even if we don't necessarily know the effect of those variables.

This chapter will focus on the concept of unsupervised machine learning and its related topics.

Moreover, this chapter will discuss some common clustering algorithms. And finally, this chapter will conclude by discussing online versus batch learning concepts.

We will divide this chapter into the following areas:

- Unsupervised learning
- Semi-supervised learning
- Anomaly detection
- Online and/or batch learning

Unsupervised learning

As we discussed in the last chapter, supervised learning is the machine learning process of leveraging a function that maps an input to an output based on example input-output pairs, inferring a function from labeled training data comprising a set of training samples.

Again, in the last chapter, we saw how, when using the model builder, we could set a **label column** for a predictive model to predict. Recall that, in one example, we chose the column IS_TENT from within the training data for the model to predict.

Now, in this section of this chapter, we want to examine scenarios where we have no label data defined in our data, or in other words, unsupervised learning problems. To reiterate, in these cases, we have no feedback (or label) based on the prior prediction results available; we expect to solve these cases without indicating or setting a desired label.

To further understand what unsupervised learning really is, you can head on to the following link: https://www.datasciencecentral.com/profiles/blogs/what-is-unsupervised-learning.

Why not always use supervised learning (and labeled data)? To understand why you might find yourself using an unsupervised learning model, consider the fact that it is usually easier to find unlabeled data (it's cheaper), and polishing unlabeled data and adding labels typically requires subject matter experts and can be a complex process in itself.

One way to accomplish the goal of unsupervised learning is through the use of a **clustering** algorithm. Clustering uses only data to determine patterns, anomalies (more on anomalies in a later section of this chapter), or similarities in the data.

Clustering organizes data by identifying data that is similar within different clusters as well as data that isn't similar across clusters.

Clustering is popular within the field of statistical data analysis as different clusters expose different details about the objects within data, which is different from classification or regression, where you have some previous information on the results.

A popular type of clustering algorithm is the **K-means clustering algorithm**. This algorithm is used to classify or to group objects based on attributes or features into *K number of groups* (indicating how the methodology got its name).

In this method, *K* will be a positive integer number and is simply the number of clusters or distinct groups the data is classified into, without the use of a labeled or target field. K-means tries to uncover patterns in the set of input fields within data rather than predicting an outcome.

In the next section of this chapter, we will look at a working example showing the use of the K-means algorithm to create clusters from data in Watson Studio in an effort to produce a prediction, without having knowledge of what the predictor(s) may be.

Watson Studio, machine learning flows, and KMeans

The **flow** editor in Watson Studio presents a very cool graphical view of a model while you build it by combining various types of nodes representing objects or actions. The flow editor has three palettes that you can choose from: SPSS modeler nodes, Spark ML algorithm nodes, and neural network nodes. In this example, we'll create an SPSS modeler flow.

Note: SPSS is the abbreviation of Statistical Package for Social Sciences and it is used by researchers to perform statistical analysis. The technology was acquired by IBM in 2009. The current versions (2015) are named IBM SPSS Statistics.

Getting started

By now, we know that you need to create a Watson project and include or add data to it. Since we've gone through this before, we'll skip over that and get into how to use the Flow Editor offered by Watson Studio.

Creating an SPSS modeler flow

Let's create an SPSS modeler flow by performing the following steps:

1. To create an SPSS modeler flow, first we must go to **Add to project**:

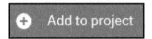

2. We can then use the **Assets** tab (as shown in the following screenshot) and click on the **Modeler Flow** icon:

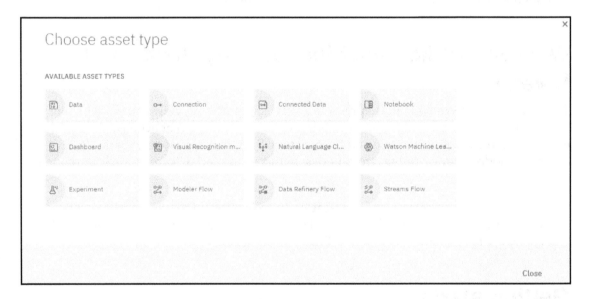

3. Next, type a name and description for the flow and select the **IBM SPSS Modeler** runtime (on the lower left) then click on the **Create** button (on the lower right):

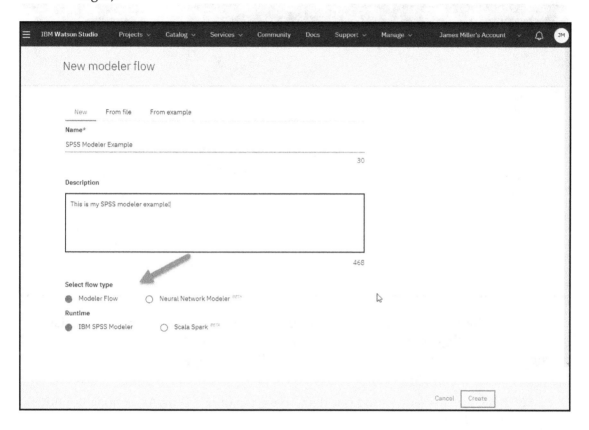

4. Now we are ready to create our machine learning modeler flow using the following flow editor canvas:

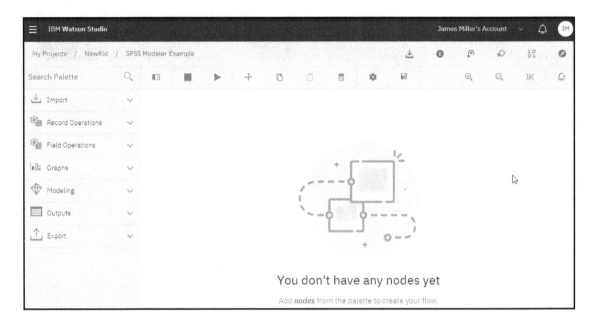

 The flow editor palette empowers you to use machine learning, **artificial intelligence (AI)**, and statistics modeling methods to derive new information from your data without the need for programming.

5. Now we are ready to add our data, so we can drag a **Data Asset** node (found under **Import**) onto the canvas:

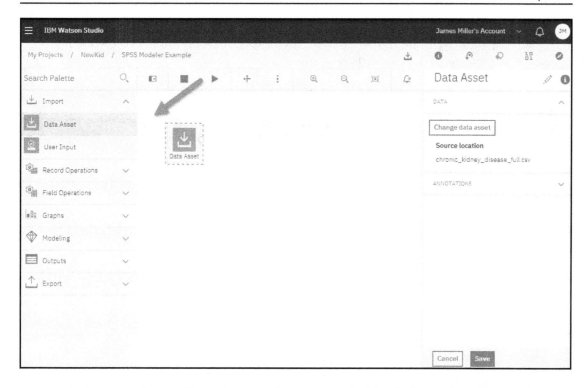

6. Once you have a **Data Asset** node, you can double-click it, select **Change data asset**, select your preferred (training) file, and then click on **OK**. If you now right-click on the node, you can select **Preview** (shown in the following screenshot) to see your data (in read-only mode):

7. To generate a profile of the data, you can add the **Data Audit** node (found under **Outputs**) by dragging it onto the canvas, connecting it to the **Data Asset** node and then clicking the VCR-type run icon:

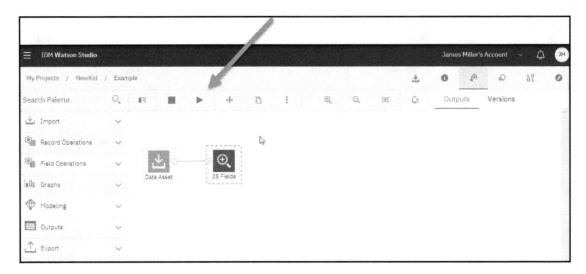

You can see that the **Data Audit** node shows **25 Fields** that it automatically found in the **Data Asset** node. Again, if you double-click on the **Data Audit** node, you'll be able to view and update various parameters, such as a name for the node (you can have multiple **Data Audit** nodes in a flow), as well as what to include in the output summarizations (graphs, basic and/or advanced statistics, and so on):

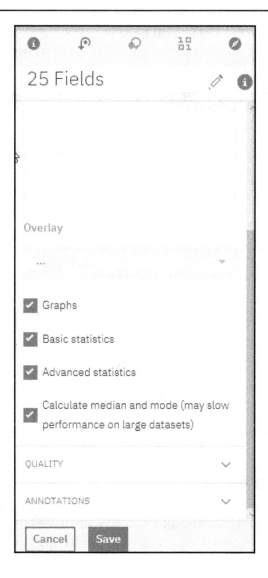

The outputs from the **Data Audit** node provides a detailed profile of your data. You can change parameters, rerun your flow, and recheck the results to become comfortable with the outputs:

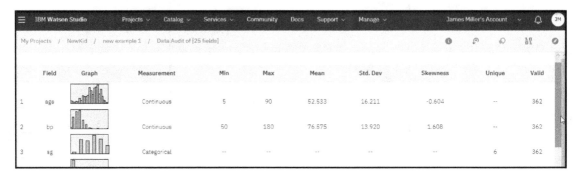

The bottom page of the preceding screenshot is as follows:

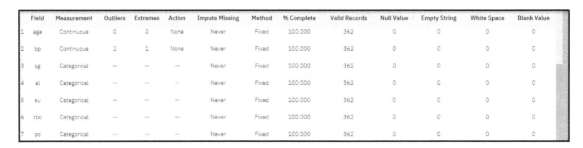

Additional node work

Before moving onto actually building a classification model, it should be noted that there are numerous nodes available on the pallet to help with or actually perform almost any operation or process that you need to perform without having to code anything!

If you take a moment to look over on the left-hand side panel (called the **Nodes Palette**), you'll see different types of nodes available for you to use while working on your data. These nodes are organized into the following six basic categories:

- **Record operations**: This can be used to perform operations such as selecting, appending, and sorting on the record (row) level.

- **Field operations**: These nodes are helpful in the data preparation phase. You can filter data, rename features, and choose the type of your attributes.
- **Graphs**: Nodes in this section will help you with basic data exploration and understanding distribution or relationship between features.
- **Modeling**: These nodes provide different modeling algorithms for different types of problems.
- **Outputs**: These nodes are helpful in understanding your data and model. You can display results in table format or get a report on evaluation parameters of your model.
- **Export**: After processing and modeling, this node will help you export data from the flow editor to your DSX project.

Let's try one out. They all are implemented in pretty much the same way: drag and drop the selected node on to the canvas and right-click to take further actions such as open, preview, or run.

For example, let's look at the **Filter** node found under **Field Operations**. The following screenshot shows the **Filter** node added to the canvas and connected to our **Data Asset** node:

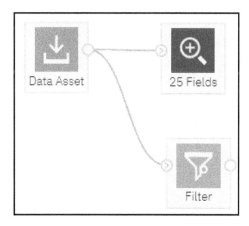

You can use the **Filter** node to rename columns, as shown in the following screenshot:

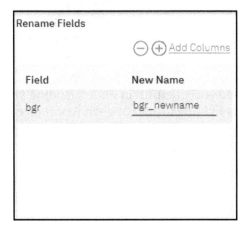

You can also filter out or retain only selected fields of data from your original **Data Asset** node:

Once you are happy with your data, you can set a variable to be the model's **Target** variable using the **Type** node. This will help the model to distinguish between input and target features. For example, you can do the following tasks:

1. Drag and drop the **Type** node on the canvas.
2. Connect the **Type** node to the **Filter** node.
3. Right-click on the **Type** node and click on **Open** to open the node.
4. Click on **Read Values**, then select the column name **class** and change the role of the variable to **Target**, and finally click on **Save**:

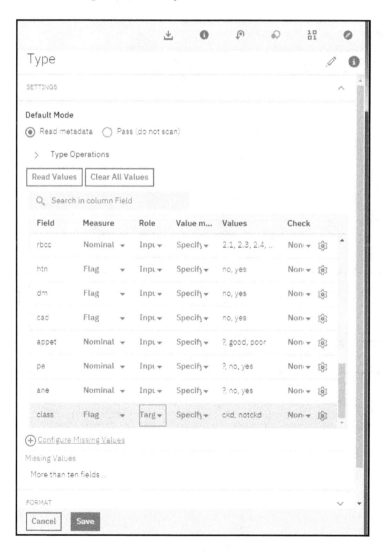

5. To see what the distribution of the **Target** variable (ours is set to **class**) is, you can use the **Distribution** node (from the **Graphs** section of the node palette). Again, just drag the node onto the canvas and open and provide information such as **Plot** (select the **class** field under **Field (discrete)**) and under **Color (discrete)** (use **class**) and click on **Save**. After you run the flow, the output looks like this:

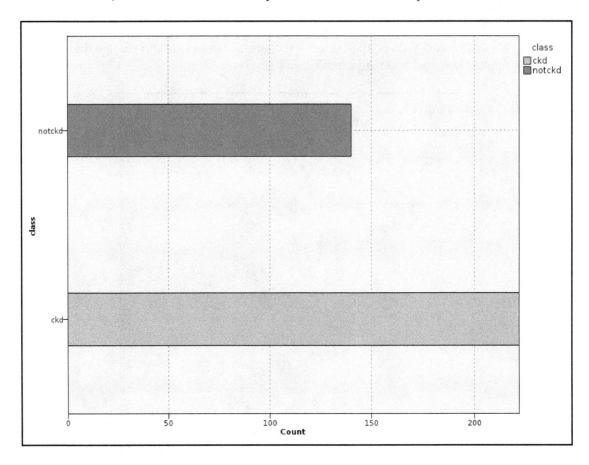

In this data, we see that there are more **cronic cases** (**ckd**) than **non-cronic cases** (**notckd**). This is our current flow displayed on the canvas:

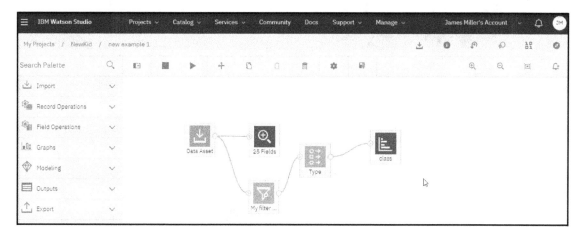

Training and testing

Another useful function in the SPSS modeler flow is the ability to easily divide data into training and testing sets. This can be accomplished using the **Partition** node. To train, test, and validate the stages of model building, the **Partition** nodes are used to produce a partition field that splits the data into separate subsets or samples.

Using a sample to generate the model and a separate sample to test it will get you a good hint of how well the model will generalize to larger datasets that are corresponding to the current data:

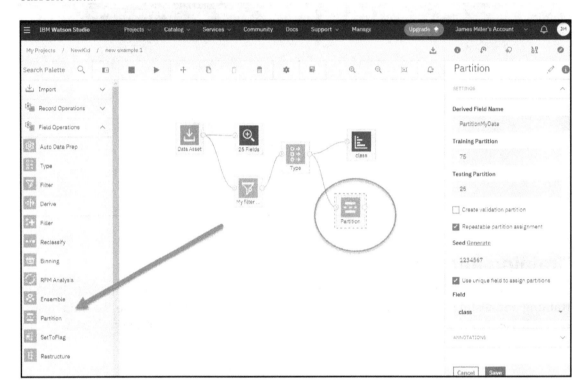

If we add a **Partition** node to our flow, open it and adjust the settings as shown in the preceding screenshot, we are instructing the modeler to add a new field (`PartionMyData`) to our data, which will designate the record split (based upon 75/25). To see the results of this node, we can add a **Table** node to the flow and provide the following settings:

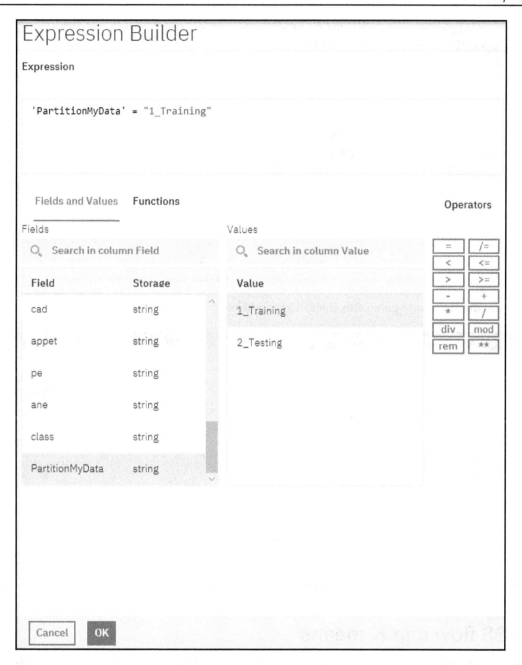

The preceding screenshot indicates that we want to query our data and generate a table based upon the values in our derived field that are equal to 1_Training; in other words, all of the records that the **Partition** node has designated as members of our training data. Our flow now looks as follows:

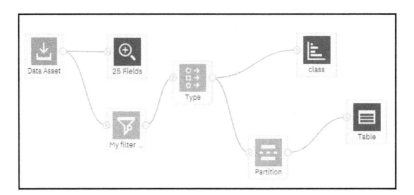

Running the flow now generates the following table:

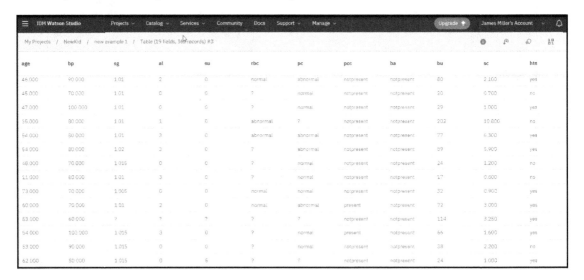

age	bp	sg	al	su	rbc	pc	pcc	ba	bu	sc	htn
48.000	90.000	1.01	2	0	normal	abnormal	notpresent	notpresent	80	2.100	yes
45.000	70.000	1.01	0	0	?	normal	notpresent	notpresent	20	0.700	no
47.000	100.000	1.01	0	0	?	normal	notpresent	notpresent	29	1.000	yes
35.000	80.000	1.01	1	0	abnormal	?	notpresent	notpresent	202	10.800	no
54.000	80.000	1.01	3	0	abnormal	abnormal	notpresent	notpresent	77	6.300	yes
54.000	80.000	1.02	3	0	?	abnormal	notpresent	notpresent	89	6.900	yes
48.000	70.000	1.015	0	0	?	normal	notpresent	notpresent	24	1.200	no
11.000	80.000	1.01	3	0	?	normal	notpresent	notpresent	17	0.800	no
73.000	70.000	1.005	0	0	normal	normal	notpresent	notpresent	32	0.900	yes
60.000	70.000	1.01	2	0	normal	abnormal	present	notpresent	72	3.000	yes
83.000	60.000	?	?	?	?	?	notpresent	notpresent	114	3.250	yes
54.000	100.000	1.015	3	0	?	normal	present	notpresent	66	1.600	yes
53.000	90.000	1.015	0	0	?	normal	notpresent	notpresent	38	2.200	no
62.000	80.000	1.015	0	5	?	?	notpresent	notpresent	24	1.000	yes

SPSS flow and K-means

As we mentioned earlier in this chapter, a popular type of clustering algorithm is the **K-means clustering** algorithm. Again, without the use of a labeled or target field, rather than trying to predict an outcome, K-means tries to uncover patterns and find structure in the data, by grouping and/or clustering data points in the set of input fields within data.

Using the sample data that we have been working with in this chapter, let's say that we don't know whether a person has chronic kidney disease or not and would like to use the K-means algorithm to build an unsupervised model to see whether we can identify any pattern for chronic kidney disease.

We'll choose the **K-Means** node in our flow to accomplish this task.

 The **K-Means** node offers a method of cluster analysis which you can refer to *Chapter 11* in the documentation of IBM SPSS Modeller 15 from the following link: `http://public.dhe.ibm.com/software/analytics/spss/documentation/modeler/15.0/en/ModelingNodes.pdf`.

Let's take a look at the following steps to learn how to learn about the K-means algorithm:

1. From the left, under **Modeling**, we can select the **K-Means** node and drop it onto the canvas.
2. Next, connect the node to the **Type** node as shown in the following screenshot:

Note that I have disconnected the **Partition** node that we used earlier.

3. Once we have added the K-Class node, right-click and open it to change its settings (on the right-hand side of the canvas). Specifically, under **BUILD OPTIONS**, we'll set **Number of clusters** to 2 based upon the idea that we would want to organize our data into two groups (or clusters): those with chronic kidney disease and those who do not have chronic kidney disease. All of the other settings can remain defaults. Finally, click on **Save**.
4. Now, after you run the flow, a golden **K-Means** node will appear (shown in the following screenshot) on which you can right-click and select **View Model**:

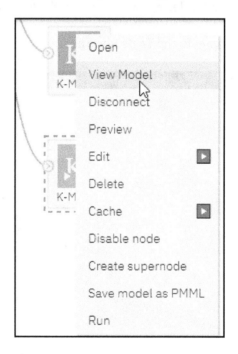

5. SPSS visualizations offer interactive tables and charts to help evaluate a predictive model. These visualizations provide a single all-inclusive set of output so that you don't need to create multiple charts and tables to determine the model's performance. Depending on the algorithm, you'll see a set of visualizations that are related to your specific data set and model. The following is the output from our K-means model:

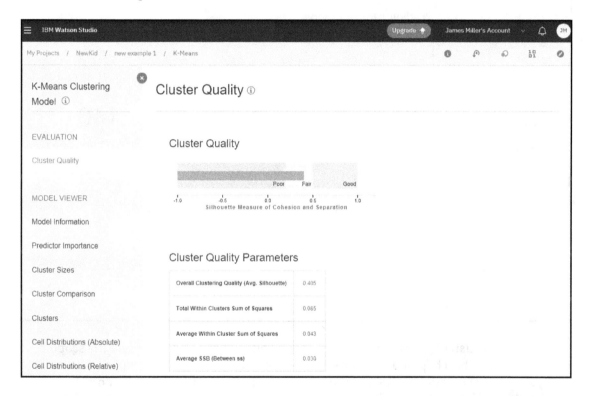

The output includes information on **Cluster Quality** (shown in the preceding screenshot) as well as **Predictor Importance** (shown in the following screenshot):

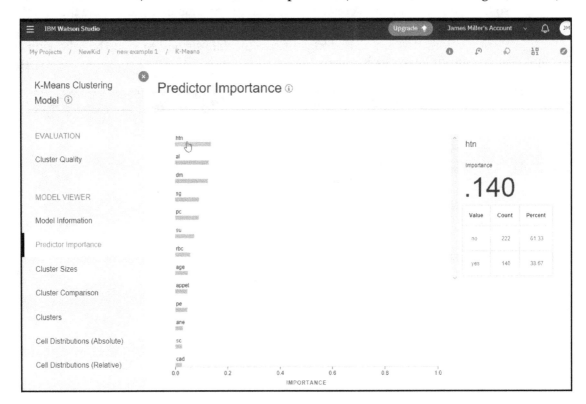

Cluster Quality Evaluation is a complex subject and is beyond the scope of this chapter, however IBM Watson Studio provides the typical Cluster Quality details such as the Cluster Sizes Chart which is a horizontal bar chart displaying the relative sizes of the clustering in descending order. Hovering over a bar shows the precise percentage of the total number of instances in that cluster based on the K-Means model. All of the clustering information should be reviewed and evaluated in respect to various project options and outcomes.

And finally (although there are other informational visualizations generated), it shows the basic **Model Information (as shown below):**

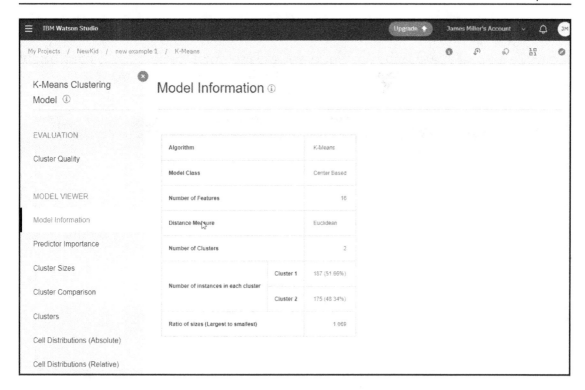

 An awesome feature of the SPSS modeler flow is that you can build multiple, different models within the same canvas!

It is literally so easily to make changes to the nodes, rerun (the flow), and then re-evaluate the results to determine the best algorithm and parameters, that you should just assume multiple iterations as part of the process.

Exporting model results

Once you are comfortable with your model, you can export the results using another handy node named the **Data Asset Export** node. As with other nodes, you can drag and drop it onto the canvas, connect it to the golden **K-Means** node and open it to edit its settings:

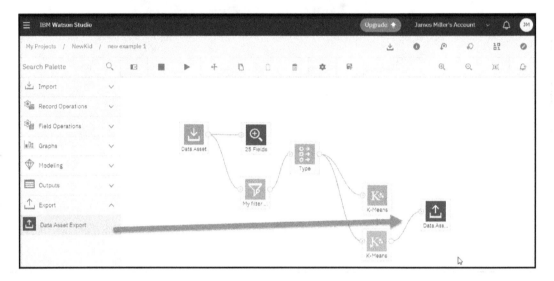

For the node settings, all you really need to do is type a name to your file (I have typed Lovely) under the **Target path** section in the **Data Asset Export** settings as shown in the following screenshot:

You might also select **Replace the data set** as the option under the **If the data set already exists*** section.

Now, when you run the flow, the data will be exported to your project storage, where you can see and access it from the **Assets** tab in the project:

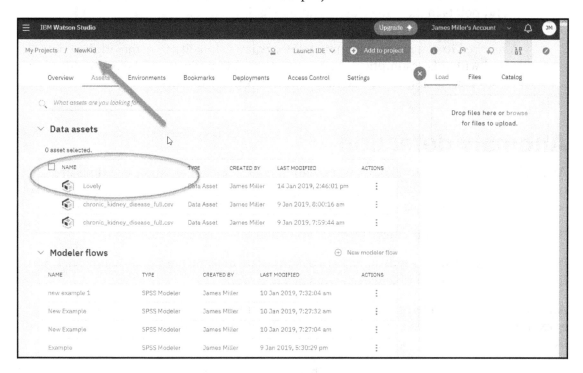

Semi-supervised learning

Semi-supervised learning is another class of machine learning process and technique that also makes use of unlabeled data for training (as does unsupervised learning) but, typically, a small amount of labeled data with a large amount of unlabeled data is present and used by the model. This is usually referred to as **partly labeled data**.

Semi-supervised learning falls somewhere between unsupervised learning (without any labeled training data) and supervised learning (with completely labeled training data).

Semi-supervised learning programs do attempt to use certain standard assumptions to help them make use of unlabeled data. These standard assumptions are continuity, cluster, and manifold.

Without going too deep into describing these assumptions, loose definitions are as follows:

- **Continuity**: This assumption implies that close data points also tends to share a label.
- **Cluster**: This assumption says that the data that tends to form discrete clusters, and points in the same cluster end up sharing a label.
- **Manifold**: This assumption assumes that the data lies approximately on what is referred to as a manifold of much lower dimensionality than the original data, and with this assumption, there is an attempt to understand the manifold using both labeled and unlabeled data to reduce dimensionality.

Anomaly detection

Anomalies also referred to as outliers, novelties, noise, deviations, and exceptions are typically defined as the identification of rare items, events, or observations within a pool or set of data that raise suspicions by differing significantly from the majority of the data.

Why should so much importance be placed on anomalies and their detection?

Because anomalies in data will almost always translate to some kind of problem, such as fraud, a defect, medical problems, or errors in a text.

Anomaly detection is a technique used to recognize unusual patterns that do not conform to expected behavior, called **outliers**. In order to locate anomalies, you need to understand that can fall into several broad categories.

Typically, we consider anomalies to be either point, contextual, or collective in nature. Point anomalies are what you may guess: a single point of data that is very different from the rest. Contextual anomalies are when seemingly good data is only good within a certain context. Collective anomalies are where you consider data in a collective set an anomaly.

Machine learning based approaches

Of course, there are a number of generally accepted machine learning based approaches to the process of anomaly detection. These currently include the following:

- **Density-based anomaly detection**: This approach is based on the KNN algorithm; the nearest set of data points are evaluated using a scoring method dependent on the type of the data (categorical or numerical).

- **Clustering-based anomaly detection**: One of the most desired concepts in the domain of unsupervised learning for anomaly detection is Clustering.
- **Support vector machine based anomaly detection**: This algorithm uses a training set to learn soft boundaries in order to cluster the normal data instances then, using the testing instance, it calibrates itself to locate the abnormalities that fall outside the learned region.

Online or batch learning

Think of online and batch machine learning concepts as basically the difference between performing multiple iterations of updating predictor values from new chunks of data compared to churning through all of the available data first, and then setting the predictor values:

- Online machine learning: This is a technique of machine learning where data are made available in sequential order and is used to streamline the best predictor for future data at each step or iteration.
- Batch learning: Batch machine learning is a method that will generate the best predictor by learning on the entire training dataset at once.

Summary

In this chapter, we started out by providing brief descriptions of unsupervised learning, semi-supervised learning, anomaly detection, and finally online and batch learning.

In the next chapter, we will use Python as the programming language on notebooks that we will learn to create. We will also learn how to create various machine learning projects with Watson Studio.

2
Section 2: Tools and Ingredients for Machine Learning in IBM Cloud

In this part of the book, you will learn about the tools and ingredients for developing practical machine learning algorithms to run in the cloud.

The following chapters will be covered in this section:

- Chapter 5, *Machine Learning Workouts on IBM Cloud*
- Chapter 6, *Using Spark with IBM Watson Studio*
- Chapter 7, *Deep Learning Using TensorFlow on the IBM Cloud*

Machine Learning Workouts on IBM Cloud

5

In this chapter, we will go through several sample machine learning (ML) exercises using the IBM Cloud platform to uncover the power of the **Python** language as the machine learning programming language of choice, and to look at the Machine Learning service offered by IBM Watson Studio.

This chapter will enable you to understand the practice of proper feature engineering as well as demonstrate the ability to run **supervised** (classification) and **unsupervised** (clustering) algorithms in the IBM Cloud, using IBM Watson Studio.

With simple practice examples, this chapter will guide you through the steps for implementing various machine learning projects using IBM Watson Studio.

We will break down this chapter into the following areas:

- Watson Studio and Python
- Data cleansing and preparation
- A k-means clustering example
- A k-nearest neighbors example
- A time series prediction example

Watson Studio and Python

As already mentioned, Python could very well be (currently anyway) the programming or scripting language most often chosen for predictive modeling and data science projects. A significant advance in the area of this type of computing is **Jupyter Notebook** (formerly, IPython) technology.

A Jupyter Notebook is a web-based environment aimed at interactive computing where you can run small bits of code to process data, and immediately view the results of that code. Notebooks include all of the building blocks you need to work with data:

- The data
- The code computations that process the data
- Visualizations of the results (of the code computations)
- Text and rich media to enhance your understanding

In addition, saved notebooks record how you worked with data, so you can more readily understand precisely what was done, reproduce those computations consistently, and even share your findings with others for collaboration.

Setting up the environment

With IBM Watson Studio, it is a pretty straightforward process to create a Python, Scala, or R notebook. These notebooks can then be used to analyze, clean, and transform data, and perform numerical simulations, statistical modeling, data visualization, machine learning, and other tasks.

To get us going with this chapter's example projects, we need to take the following steps to create a new project and add a notebook in IBM Watson Studio:

1. Create a new project by first clicking on **New project**; then, from the **Create a project** page (shown as follows), find **Deep Learning** and then click on **Create Project**:

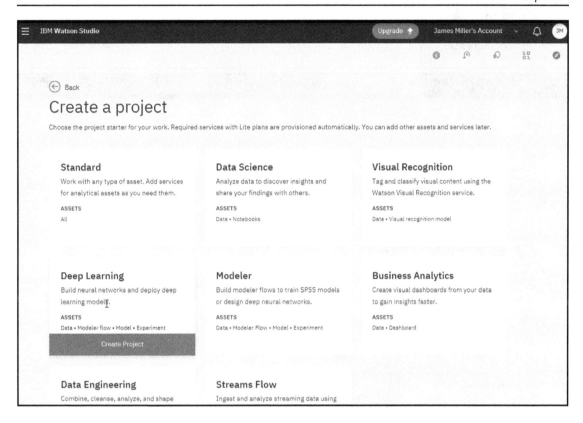

2. Next, select a region for the machine learning service to run in then click on **Select**:

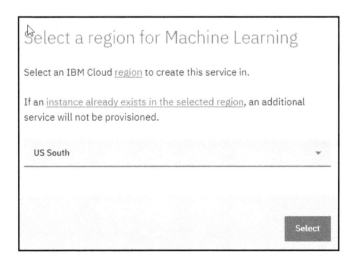

3. Name your project on the **New project** page (shown as follows), and then click on **Create**:

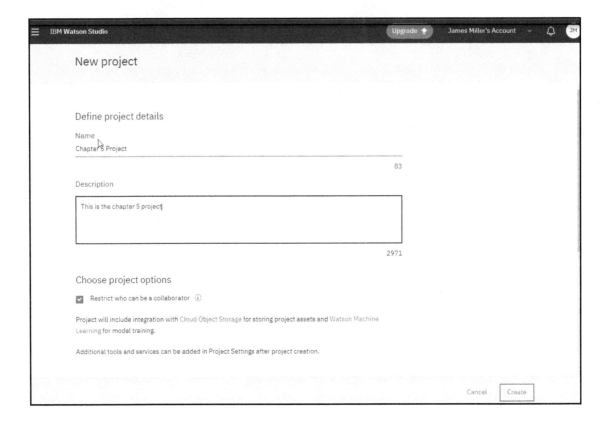

4. Now that we have created a machine learning project, we are ready to create a notebook. Notebooks are considered a project asset that can be used and shared. To create a notebook from within the project, you click on **Add to project**:

5. Once you have clicked **Add to project,** you need to choose an asset type. In previous examples, we selected the **DATA** and **DASHBOARD** asset types; here we will choose **NOTEBOOK**:

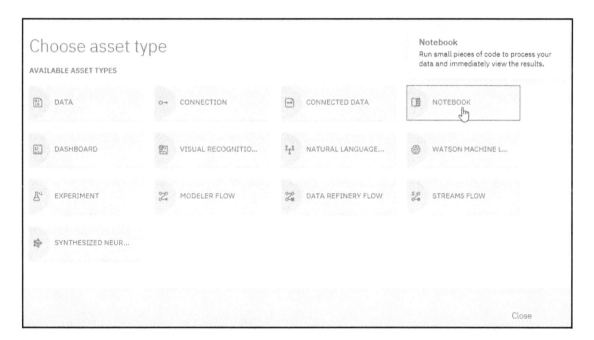

6. Like creating projects, once you select **NOTEBOOK** as the asset type, you need to provide a name and description under the **Name** and **Description** options for the new notebook:

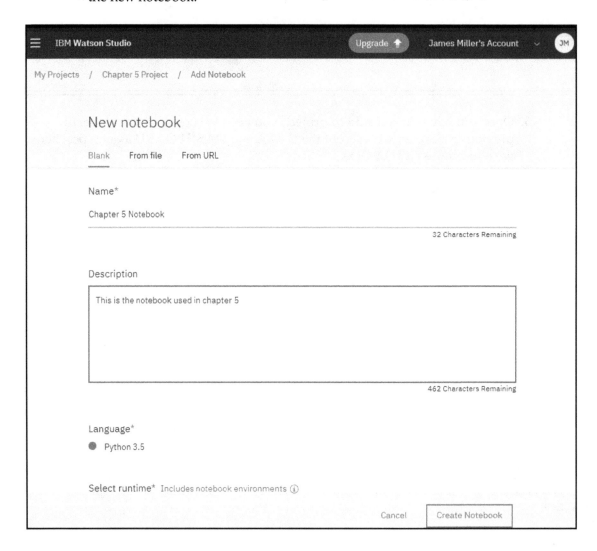

7. In addition, in the bottom left-hand of the page, you will need to select a language for the notebook to use. Notice that the default is Python 3.5:

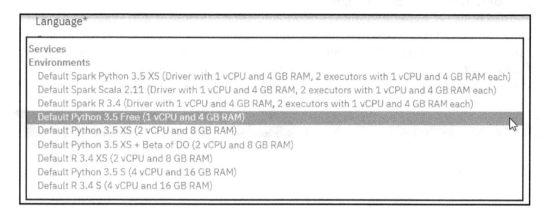

8. Since we will use Python in our examples, we can simply click on **Create Notebook**. Take note that IBM Watson Studio notebooks (currently) support the following runtime languages. Once you click on **Create Notebook**, the notebook instance will be created and initialized for use:

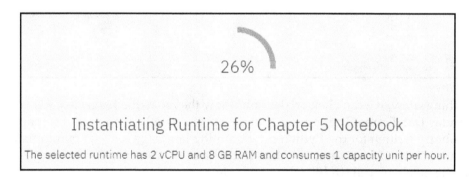

Try it out

Once your notebook has been instantiated, you are ready to run Python commands and code. Take notice of a couple of things in the following screenshot. For example, we have entered a snip of Python code in the first **cell** of the notebook that iterates with a for loop and prints columns of data. The other thing to notice is that we have clicked on **Find and add data** and added a new file (**winemag-data-130k-v2.csv**) as an asset, as shown in the following screenshot:

To make things easy, we can click on the link below the file name **Insert to code** and select **Insert pandas DataFrame**. The result is that the appropriate **Python** modules (pandas is a software library written for the Python programming language for data manipulation and analysis) are imported for us and a Python DataFrame is automatically defined. This is shown in the notebook cell (**In [9]**) in the following screenshot:

```
In [9]:
import types
import pandas as pd
from botocore.client import Config
import ibm_boto3

def __iter__(self): return 0

# @hidden_cell
# The following code accesses a file in your IBM Cloud Object Storage. It includes your credentials.
# You might want to remove those credentials before you share your notebook.
client_f20250362df648648ee81858c2a341b5 = ibm_boto3.client(service_name='s3',
    ibm_api_key_id='dkLHOXeBL-LhRRALaKACqdqFXWDlCd32BsfOndx1xFpy',
    ibm_auth_endpoint="https://iam.bluemix.net/oidc/token",
    config=Config(signature_version='oauth'),
    endpoint_url='https://s3-api.us-geo.objectstorage.service.networklayer.com')

body = client_f20250362df648648ee81858c2a341b5.get_object(Bucket='chapter5project-donotdelete-pr-qisyarw87xi
# add missing __iter__ method, so pandas accepts body as file-like object
if not hasattr(body, "__iter__"): body.__iter__ = types.MethodType( __iter__, body )

df_data_1 = pd.read_csv(body)
df_data_1.head()
```

The output generated by the last line of code, `df_data_1.head()` is displayed in the notebook cell **Out [9]**:

Out[9]:

	Unnamed: 0	country	description	designation	points	price	province	region_1	region_2	taster_name	taster_twitter_handle
0	0	Italy	Aromas include tropical fruit, broom, brimston...	Vulkà Bianco	87	NaN	Sicily & Sardinia	Etna	NaN	Kerin O'Keefe	@kerinokeefe
1	1	Portugal	This is ripe and fruity, a wine that is smooth...	Avidagos	87	15.0	Douro	NaN	NaN	Roger Voss	@vossroger
2	2	US	Tart and snappy, the flavors of lime flesh and...	NaN	87	14.0	Oregon	Willamette Valley	Willamette Valley	Paul Gregutt	@paulgwine

Now we have a data asset (a CVS file) loaded and accessible in our Watson Studio project via a DataFrame object.

Data cleansing and preparation

A common description for data cleansing and preparation is the work that goes into transforming **raw data** into a form that data scientists and analysts can more easily run through machine learning algorithms in an effort to uncover insights or make predictions based upon that data.

This process can be complicated by issues such as missing or incomplete records or simply finding extraneous columns of information within a data source.

In the previous example screenshot, we can see that the DataFrame object includes the columns **country**, **description**, **designation**, **points**, **price**, **province**, and so on.

As an exercise designed to demonstrate how easily we can use Python within Watson Studio to prepare data, let's suppose that we wanted to drop one or more columns from the DataFrame. To accomplish this task, we use the following Python statements:

```
to_drop = ['points']
df_data_1.drop(to_drop, inplace=True, axis=1)
df_data_1.head()
```

The preceding simple Python commands define the column name to be dropped from the DataFrame, that is, **points** and then drop the column from the df_data_1 DataFrame:

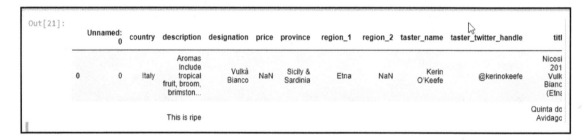

Within IBM Watson Studio, using the notebook we created earlier in this chapter, we can enter and run the preceding commands, and then use the head() function, to verify that the column we indicated has actually been dropped.

Although the preceding demonstration is simplistic and doesn't begin to break the surface on the process of data cleansing and preparation, it does demonstrate the ability to use Python easily in Watson Studio to access and manipulate data.

Rather than continuing with additional fundamental data manipulations, we'll move on to looking at something a bit more complex.

K-means clustering using Python

To recap from `Chapter 4`, *Machine Learning Workouts on IBM Cloud*, **k-means clustering** is an unsupervised machine learning methodology—an algorithm that is commonly used to find groups within **unlabeled** data. Again, since the goal here is to demonstrate how you can apply this methodology to some data using Python in Watson Studio, we won't bother to dissect the details of how k-means works, but will show a working example of the algorithm, using Watson Studio as a proof of concept.

There are numerous examples available online and elsewhere demonstrating the use of Python to implement k-means logic. Here, we'll use an example that is simple to follow and uses available Python modules, such as `matplotlib`, `pandas`, and `scipy`.

Our exercise, using IBM Watson Studio and the Notebook (we created in the sections of this chapter) will:

1. Create a DataFrame for a two-dimensional dataset
2. Find centroids for three clusters, and then for four clusters
3. Add a **graphical user interface (GUI)** to display the results

 The most representative point within a group is called the **centroid**. It is defined as the mean of the values of the points of **data** in the cluster. Each cluster should consist of the points of **data** closest to it.

The Python code

First, we can take a look at the Python code:

1. This step references `pandas` and then defines our two-dimensional DataFrame. Note that the data is simply two lists of numbers, defined as `x` and `y`:

```
from pandas import DataFrame
Data = {'x':
[25,34,22,27,33,33,31,22,35,34,67,54,57,43,50,57,59,52,65,47,49,48,
35,33,44,45,38,43,51,46],
        'y':
[79,51,53,78,59,74,73,57,69,75,51,32,40,47,53,36,35,58,59,50,25,20,
14,12,20,5,29,27,8,7]
        }
df = DataFrame(Data,columns=['x','y'])
print (df)
```

The last command (`print(df)`) is added so that if you run the code, you'll get to see the output, which should match the dataset that was defined.

2. The next step is where we will use the `sklearn` Python module to find the centroids for three and then for four clusters, and the `matplotlib` module to create some charts to visualize the results of the algorithm.

 Scikit-learn provides a range of supervised as well as unsupervised learning algorithms through a consistent interface in Python. The library is built upon the SciPy (Scientific Python). **Matplotlib** is a plotting library for Python and its numerical mathematics extension NumPy (Wikipedia, 2019).

3. Once the DataFrame is created using the columns of data entered, the next block of Python code also imports the two aforementioned Python modules and specifies the number of clusters to create with the `KMeans` algorithm and finally uses `matplotlib` to generate some scatter plots:

```
from pandas import DataFrame
import matplotlib.pyplot as plt
from sklearn.cluster import KMeans
Data = {'x':
[25,34,22,27,33,33,31,22,35,34,67,54,57,43,50,57,59,52,65,47,49,48,
35,33,44,45,38,43,51,46],
        'y':
[79,51,53,78,59,74,73,57,69,75,51,32,40,47,53,36,35,58,59,50,25,20,
14,12,20,5,29,27,8,7]
        }
df = DataFrame(Data,columns=['x','y'])
kmeans = KMeans(n_clusters=3).fit(df)
centroids = kmeans.cluster_centers_
print(centroids)
plt.scatter(df['x'], df['y'], c= kmeans.labels_.astype(float),
s=50, alpha=0.5)
plt.scatter(centroids[:, 0], centroids[:, 1], c='red', s=50)
plt.show()
```

The output from the preceding Python code generates the following output:

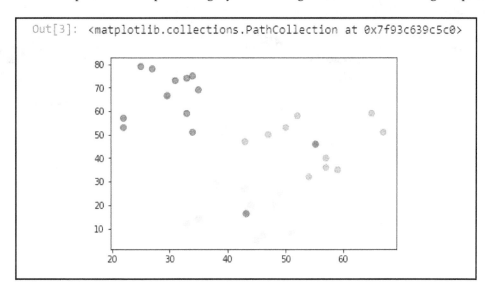

```
Out[3]:   <matplotlib.collections.PathCollection at 0x7f93c639c5c0>
```

Observing the results

Note that the center of each of the three clusters (in red) represents the mean of all the observations that belong to that cluster. As you might also see, the observations that belong to a given cluster are closer to the center of that cluster, in comparison to the centers of other clusters.

Implementing in Watson

Again, rather than dwell on the interpretation of the previous output, let's look at how we might be able to implement the same exercise using IBM Watson Studio. We could use the Notebook we created earlier in this chapter, but let's create a fresh new one (following the same procedure as we used earlier).

Once the Notebook is open and ready, we can run the Python code we just reviewed. First paste the original code block into the first Notebook cell and click on **Run**:

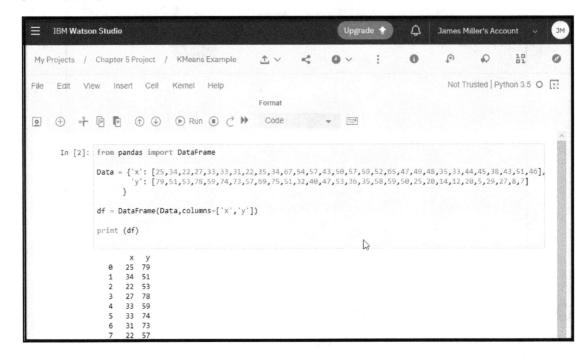

Repeat the step but with the following code block:

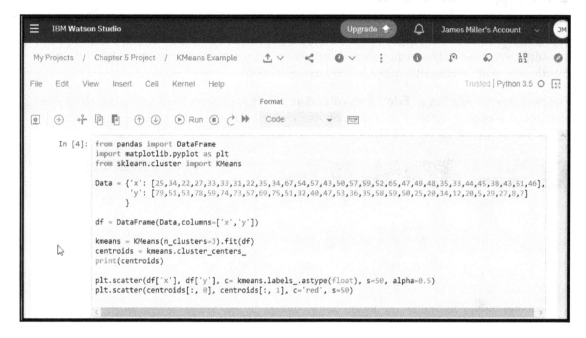

This yields the following output:

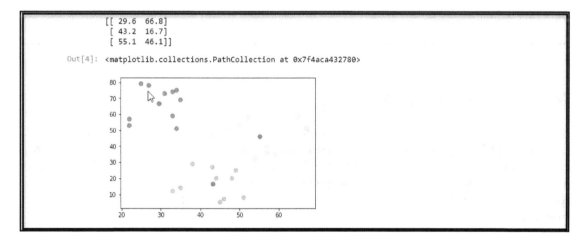

Saving your work

Once you are satisfied with the results, you should save your Notebook by clicking on **File** and then **Save**. Additionally, a nice feature is the ability to download the Notebook in various formats so that you can share with others who may not have access to Watson Studio. We will discuss this more in the next section.

For now, try navigating to **File** | **Download as** | **Python (.py)**, which will save all of the Python code blocks within the Notebook as a standard Python code file, which can be shared and run within other Python environments:

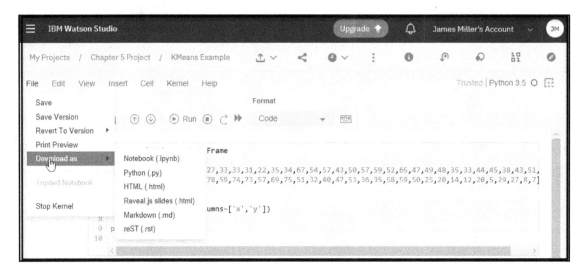

K-nearest neighbors

As the previous algorithm (KMeans) is an **unsupervised** learning methodology, the **k-nearest neighbors** (**KNN**) algorithm is a fundamentally simple to understand **supervised** machine learning methodology. The concept of the KNN algorithm is described commonly as classifying data by identifying its nearest neighbor or, my favorite analogy, you can identify or classify data by identifying who it associates most with or finding its closest neighbor.

The Python code

As we stated earlier, our objective is to demonstrate how to implement various types of ML algorithms within IBM Watson Studio, not provide the theory behind each algorithm; in addition to that, consistent with the last section, we will utilize an existing sample Python script set to illustrate the functionalities and features offered within the Watson Studio platform, and not try to create a new solution.

In this implemented example, we have to do the following:

- Find a predefined number of training samples closest in distance to a new sample of data that needs to be classified
- Make sure the label (classification) of the new sample of data is defined by those (training sample) neighbors
- Set a fixed user-defined constant for the number of neighbors that have to be determined
- Compute the classification using a majority vote of the nearest neighbors of the new sample

Implementing in Watson

Once again, following the steps used earlier in this chapter, we can open our machine learning project in IBM Watson Studio and create a new Notebook. From there, we can paste the sample Python code into cells within the Notebook and press **Run** to test each cell's code.

As we've seen, you can use multiple cells within the Notebook to segment functional blocks of your code. Using the menu bar, you can also cut and paste cells, split and merge cells, and move a cell up or down within the Notebook. For clarity, an additional handy feature is to display the line numbers for each of the Python commands in the Notebook. You can do this by clicking the appropriate menu selection under **Edit** or **View** on the menu bar:

You may want to split cells to show intermediate cell outputs or combine cells into one cell and show the combined output. For example, in the next screenshot, you can see two cells, each followed by their respective outputs:

```
In [1]:   1  import numpy as np
          2  from sklearn import datasets
          3  iris = datasets.load_iris()
          4  iris_data = iris.data
          5  iris_labels = iris.target
          6  print(iris_data[0], iris_data[79], iris_data[100])
          7  print(iris_labels[0], iris_labels[79], iris_labels[100])

          [ 5.1  3.5  1.4  0.2] [ 5.7  2.6  3.5  1. ] [ 6.3  3.3  6.    2.5]
          0 1 2
```

```
In [2]:   1  np.random.seed(42)
          2  indices = np.random.permutation(len(iris_data))
          3  n_training_samples = 12
          4  learnset_data = iris_data[indices[:-n_training_samples]]
          5  learnset_labels = iris_labels[indices[:-n_training_samples]]
          6  testset_data = iris_data[indices[-n_training_samples:]]
          7  testset_labels = iris_labels[indices[-n_training_samples:]]
          8  print(learnset_data[:4], learnset_labels[:4])
          9  print(testset_data[:4], testset_labels[:4])

          [[ 6.1  2.8  4.7  1.2]
           [ 5.7  3.8  1.7  0.3]
           [ 7.7  2.6  6.9  2.3]
           [ 6.   2.9  4.5  1.5]] [1 0 2 1]
          [[ 5.7  2.8  4.1  1.3]
           [ 6.5  3.   5.5  1.8]
           [ 6.3  2.3  4.4  1.3]
           [ 6.4  2.9  4.3  1.3]] [1 2 1 1]
```

The following screenshot shows those two cells combined into one followed by the combined output:

```
In [5]:    1  import numpy as np
           2  from sklearn import datasets
           3  iris = datasets.load_iris()
           4  iris_data = iris.data
           5  iris_labels = iris.target
           6  print(iris_data[0], iris_data[79], iris_data[100])
           7  print(iris_labels[0], iris_labels[79], iris_labels[100])
           8
           9  np.random.seed(42)
          10  indices = np.random.permutation(len(iris_data))
          11  n_training_samples = 12
          12  learnset_data = iris_data[indices[:-n_training_samples]]
          13  learnset_labels = iris_labels[indices[:-n_training_samples]]
          14  testset_data = iris_data[indices[-n_training_samples:]]
          15  testset_labels = iris_labels[indices[-n_training_samples:]]
          16  print(learnset_data[:4], learnset_labels[:4])
          17  print(testset_data[:4], testset_labels[:4])

[ 5.1  3.5  1.4  0.2] [ 5.7  2.6  3.5  1. ] [ 6.3  3.3  6.    2.5]
0 1 2
[[ 6.1  2.8  4.7  1.2]
 [ 5.7  3.8  1.7  0.3]
 [ 7.7  2.6  6.9  2.3]
 [ 6.   2.9  4.5  1.5]] [1 0 2 1]
[[ 5.7  2.8  4.1  1.3]
 [ 6.5  3.   5.5  1.8]
 [ 6.3  2.3  4.4  1.3]
 [ 6.4  2.9  4.3  1.3]] [1 2 1 1]
```

Using the menu options, you can create a very well-organized, functional, and sharable solution. In the next section, we will use **Markdown tags** within Watson Studio to create an even more valuable solution.

Exploring Markdown text

Markdown is an easily-used markup language that is used with plain text to add formatting elements (headings, bulleted lists, URLs, and so on) to plain text without the use of a formal text editor or the use of **HTML** tags. Markdown is device agnostic and displays the writing format consistently across device types in an effort to create visual interest in the Notebook solutions you create.

Let's complete our latest example case. We'll assume that all of the example Python code has been pasted into cells in the Notebook and we have run the solution in its entirety.

Now, suppose that we want to save and share this solution with others who are not familiar with our project and our thought process? What we can do is insert additional cells within our Notebook and instead of pasting code into them, we can add comments and other information as explanatory text so that others can more easily understand what we have created. For example, take a look at the following screenshot:

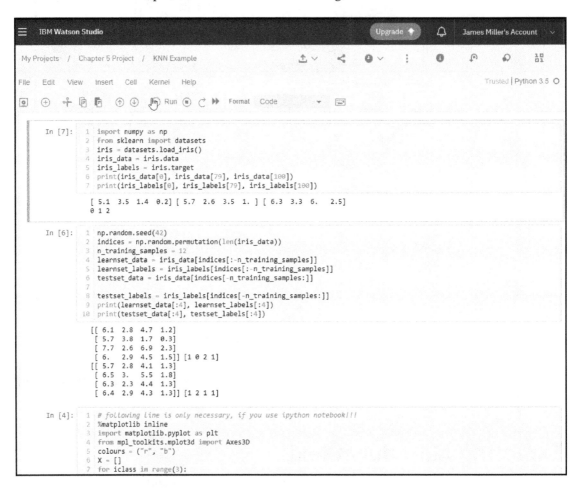

Let's see how this is done by performing the following steps:

1. We can click on the first cell in the Notebook and then click on **Insert**, then **Insert Cell Above**. Next click on the new cell and change the **Format** (of the cell) to **Markdown**:

2. Next, enter the `k-Nearest-Neighbor Classifier` text into the new cell:

```
k-Nearest-Neighbor Classifier
```

3. Then, click on the keyboard icon and select **change cell to heading 1**:

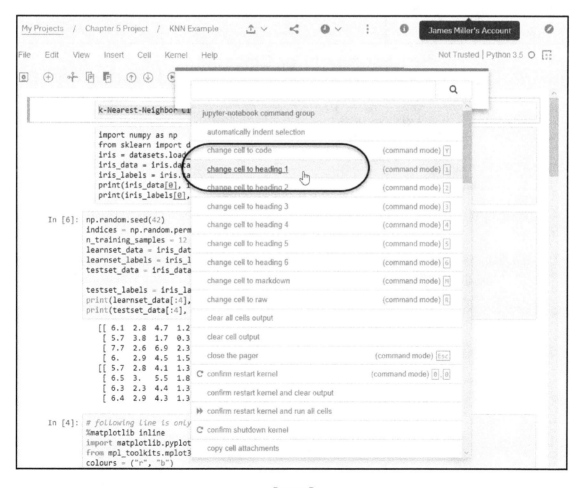

4. After you perform the preceding steps, you can see that the Markdown cell looks a bit different:

5. Once you click on **Run**, you can see the results:

Using common Markdown, we can proceed to interject commentary throughout the Notebook:

- You can add a new cell to the top of the Notebook, convert the format to Markdown, then drag and drop an image to the cell (as shown below). This can be used to add a company logo or even a workflow diagram:

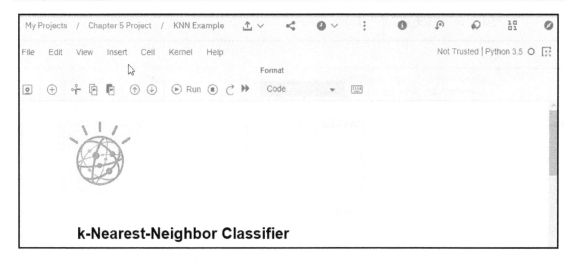

k-Nearest-Neighbor Classifier

- Using other markdowns, such as heading levels, indents, and bulleted lists, you can provide details about assumptions, such as the source of the data used and what is found within the data:

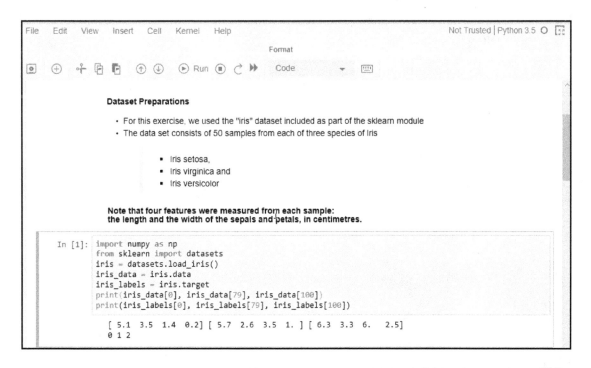

- Using additional, HTML-like markdowns (such as `<font color=></font>`), you can create markdown cells such as the following:

```
##### <font color=green>The following code is only necessary to visualize the data of our
learnset. Our data consists of four values per iris item, so we will reduce the data to three
values by summing up the third and fourth value. This way, we are capable of depicting the data
in 3-dimensional space:</font>
```

This results in the following output:

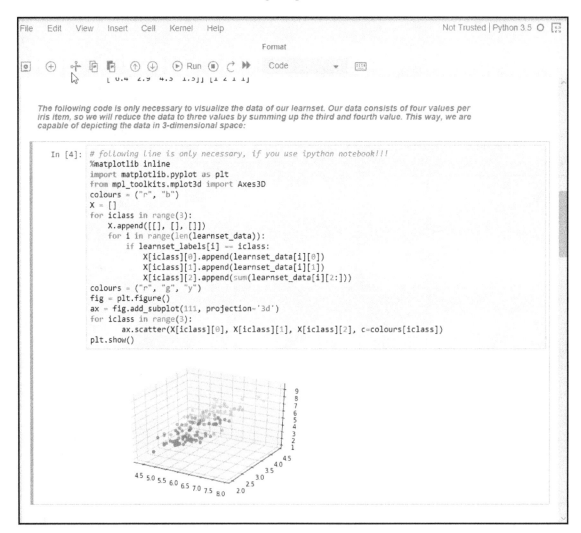

You can experiment with the full-featured Markdowns to see what works best for you. You can go to: `https://commonmark.org/help/` to find a full Markdown cheatsheet.

Time series prediction example

In this section, our goal is to try implementing a time series model using Python and Watson Studio.

Time series analysis includes methods for analyzing time series data (of course) so we can extract meaningful statistics and other characteristics of the data. Time series forecasting is the process where we use an algorithm to predict future values based on previously observed values.

Time series analysis

Time series data may be **stationary** or **non-stationary** in nature. Stationary implies flat without periodic fluctuations, while non-stationary data typically has frequent shifts in value. You see time series analysis generally used for non-stationary data, such as evaluating and predicting retail sales. In this example, we will again utilize a study exercise (available on GitHub) to demonstrate the fundamental steps involved in the analysis and forecasting of retail sales data, as implemented with IBM Watson Studio.

Setup

Using the (now) familiar process of adding data to our Watson Studio project, we've created a new asset using a CSV data file and, in an effort to better understand the data, used the Data Refinery feature to analyze, profile, and visualize our asset. From there (as we did in a previous *Time series analysis* section of this chapter), we used **Insert to Code** and then **Insert pandas DataFrame** so that Watson Studio would generate the code required to import the required Python modules, load the data (into a Python DataFrame object, named `df_data_1`) and print the first five rows, as shown in the following screenshot:

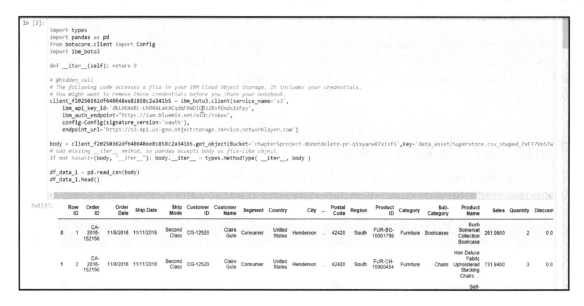

Data preprocessing

While using the **Data Refinery** feature, we noticed that there is a column within the data file named `Category`, which seems to indicate the type of product sold (furniture, office supplies, and several others). In this example, the data scientist is interested in only furniture sales, so the following lines of code are used to filter the data and then verify if there is a reasonable amount of data for that category to perform a proper analysis:

```
furniture = df.loc[df['Category'] == 'Furniture']
furniture['Order Date'].min(), furniture['Order Date'].max()
```

The preceding code executed in Watson Studio is shown in the following screenshot, filtering the sales data and verifying that we have four years of furniture sales within this data file by showing the earliest and latest timestamp:

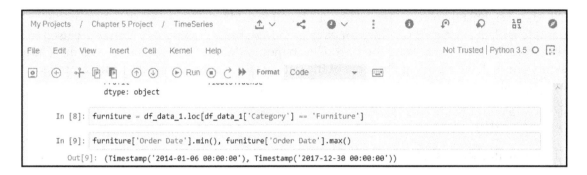

In the selected example, the data scientist chose to use raw Python commands to remove (drop) columns of data not needed in the analysis, check for missing values, aggregate (group by) sales transactions by date, and so on. Although using Python scripting to accomplish these tasks is not overly complex, you can alternatively perform all of those tasks (and more) with the drag and drop of Watson **Data Refinery flow**.

As we mentioned earlier, a Data Refinery flow is an ordered set of steps to cleanse, shape, and enhance a data asset. As you refine data by applying operations to the data, you are actually dynamically building a customized Data Refinery flow that can be modified in real time and saved for future use as new data becomes available!

Indexing for visualization

Once the data has been properly prepared, the data scientist uses the `Pandas set_index` command to set the `Order Date` column, indexing the rows (of sales transactions) as the field we will perform the initial analysis on. In other words, we want to ultimately be able to predict furniture sales per month. The following screenshot shows the Python statements executed in our Watson project to set the index and print the results of the command:

```
In [15]:  furniture = furniture.set_index('Order Date')
          furniture.index

Out[15]:  DatetimeIndex(['2014-01-06', '2014-01-07', '2014-01-10', '2014-01-11',
                         '2014-01-13', '2014-01-14', '2014-01-16', '2014-01-19',
                         '2014-01-20', '2014-01-21',
                         ...
                         '2017-12-18', '2017-12-19', '2017-12-21', '2017-12-22',
                         '2017-12-23', '2017-12-24', '2017-12-25', '2017-12-28',
                         '2017-12-29', '2017-12-30'],
                        dtype='datetime64[ns]', name='Order Date', length=889, freq=None)
```

The data scientist then goes on to point out that it would be more reasonable (given the data) to look at average daily sales for each month, so the following commands are used to **resample** the sales data, using the start of each month (MS) as the timestamp, and then, as a sanity check, have a peek at the some of the data (order month followed by the computed average sales):

```
y = furniture['Sales'].resample('MS').mean()
y["2017":]
```

The following screenshot shows the preceding commands executed in our Watson project:

```
Out[18]:  Order Date
          2017-01-01     397.602133
          2017-02-01     528.179800
          2017-03-01     544.672240
          2017-04-01     453.297905
          2017-05-01     678.302328
          2017-06-01     826.460291
          2017-07-01     562.524857
          2017-08-01     857.881889
          2017-09-01    1209.508583
          2017-10-01     875.362728
          2017-11-01    1277.817759
          2017-12-01    1256.298672
          Freq: MS, Name: Sales, dtype: float64
```

Visualizations

To actually visualize the average sales volumes over the 4-year series, the `plot` command is used:

```
y.plot(figsize=(15, 6))
plt.show()
```

This results in the following visualization, shown here executed in Watson Studio:

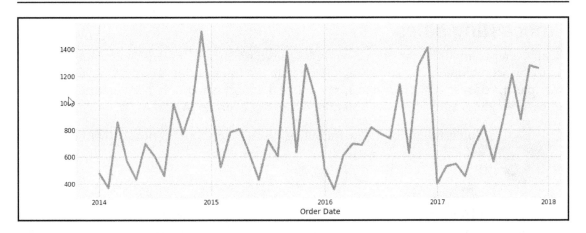

When you plot or otherwise visualize data, it is much easier to recognize patterns. In this example, the data scientist pointed out a pattern commonly identified as seasonality. The data scientist then goes a step further and performs a time series decomposition, breaking out trend, seasonality, and noise, using the following commands:

```
from pylab import rcParams
rcParams['figure.figsize'] = 18, 8
decomposition = sm.tsa.seasonal_decompose(y, model='additive')
fig = decomposition.plot()
plt.show()
```

And again, as executed in Watson Studio, we have the following:

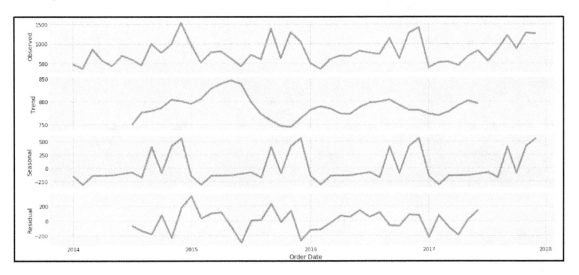

Forecasting sales

Finally, after completing the preceding time series data analysis and decomposition, we can get to the actual forecasting step! Still in-step with the track outlined in the selected example, the data scientist chose to apply one of the most commonly used methods for time series forecasting, **autoregressive integrated moving average (ARIMA)**.

 You can head on to the following link to learn more about ARIMA: `http:/ /www.forecastingsolutions.com/arima.html`.

To use an ARIMA model or methodology for a time series forecasting exercise, you'll need to understand how to choose values for the algorithms' three main parameters: as P, D, and Q. Assuming you've validated your model choice (to use ARIMA in the first place), the hardest part of building the actual forecasting model and generating a forecast with the model is selecting those parameter values that best fit the model (given the data):

- P is the number of autoregressive terms
- D is the number of nonseasonal differences needed for stationarity
- Q is the number of lagged forecast errors in the prediction equation

Without digging too deep into the theories behind parameter selection, we'll say here that this step involves determining the possible parameter value combinations, looking at their overall fitting results, running the appropriate diagnostics to investigate any unusual behaviors by the model, and validating results generated by the model.

The following are the code blocks and selected outputs as implemented with IBM Watson Studio:

Let's take a look at the first code here that shows the examples of the parameter combinations:

```
In [19]: p = d = q = range(0, 2)
         pdq = list(itertools.product(p, d, q))
         seasonal_pdq = [(x[0], x[1], x[2], 12) for x in list(itertools.product(p, d, q))]

         print('Examples of parameter combinations for Seasonal ARIMA...')
         print('SARIMAX: {} x {}'.format(pdq[1], seasonal_pdq[1]))
         print('SARIMAX: {} x {}'.format(pdq[1], seasonal_pdq[2]))
         print('SARIMAX: {} x {}'.format(pdq[2], seasonal_pdq[3]))
         print('SARIMAX: {} x {}'.format(pdq[2], seasonal_pdq[4]))

         Examples of parameter combinations for Seasonal ARIMA...
         SARIMAX: (0, 0, 1) x (0, 0, 1, 12)
         SARIMAX: (0, 0, 1) x (0, 1, 0, 12)
         SARIMAX: (0, 1, 0) x (0, 1, 1, 12)
         SARIMAX: (0, 1, 0) x (1, 0, 0, 12)
```

Let's take a look at the next code here:

```
In [20]: for param in pdq:
             for param_seasonal in seasonal_pdq:
                 try:
                     mod = sm.tsa.statespace.SARIMAX(y,
                                                     order=param,
                                                     seasonal_order=param_seasonal,
                                                     enforce_stationarity=False,
                                                     enforce_invertibility=False)

                     results = mod.fit()

                     print('ARIMA{}x{}12 - AIC:{}'.format(param, param_seasonal, results.aic))
                 except:
                     continue
```

Now, take a look at the following screenshot:

```
In [21]: mod = sm.tsa.statespace.SARIMAX(y,
                                         order=(1, 1, 1),
                                         seasonal_order=(1, 1, 0, 12),
                                         enforce_stationarity=False,
                                         enforce_invertibility=False)

         results = mod.fit()

         print(results.summary().tables[1])

         ==============================================================================
                          coef    std err          z      P>|z|      [0.025      0.975]
         ------------------------------------------------------------------------------
         ar.L1          0.0146      0.342      0.043      0.966      -0.655       0.684
         ma.L1         -1.0000      0.360     -2.781      0.005      -1.705      -0.295
         ar.S.L12      -0.0253      0.042     -0.609      0.543      -0.107       0.056
         sigma2      2.958e+04   1.22e-05   2.43e+09      0.000    2.96e+04    2.96e+04
         ==============================================================================
```

Now, let's take a look at all the graphs here at once:

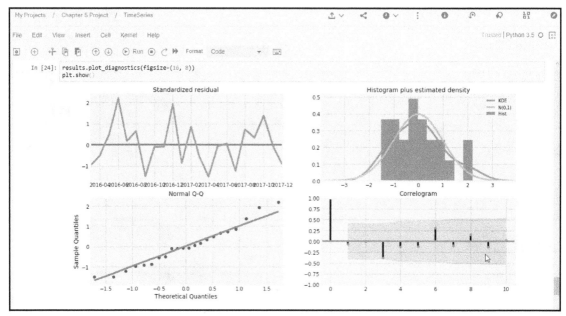

Validation

Of course, the data scientist cannot generate a forecast and be done. An effort must be made to review the model's performance or forecast accuracy. To help understand the accuracy of the model, *predicted* sales are compared to actual sales, setting the forecast to start at 2017-07-01 (to the end of the data). Again, a plot is used to visualize the output, showing the *observed* values compared to the rolling forecast predictions. Overall, the sales forecast seems to align with the actual sales values and shows an upward trend that starts from the beginning of the year.

We see the following code block:

```
pred = results.get_prediction(start=pd.to_datetime('2017-01-01'),
dynamic=False)
pred_ci = pred.conf_int()
ax = y['2014':].plot(label='observed')
pred.predicted_mean.plot(ax=ax, label='One-step' ahead Forecast', alpha=.7,
figsize=(14, 7))
ax.fill_between(pred_ci.index, pred_ci.iloc[:, 0], pred_ci.iloc[:, 1],
color='k', alpha)
ax.set_xlabel('Date')
```

```
ax.set_ylabel('Furniture Sales')
plt.legend()
plt.show()
```

The actual results implemented in Watson Studio are as follows:

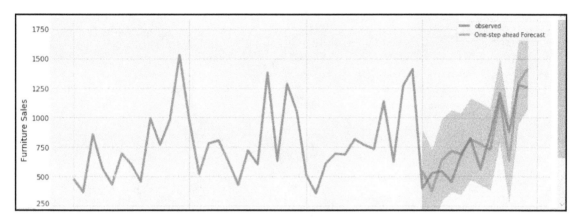

Summary

In this chapter, we created a new machine learning project in IBM Watson Studio and added notebooks to it so that we could use Python as the programming language for our project's objectives.

Using Python, we demonstrated how easy it is to load data into a DataFrame and perform manipulations on it in preparation for further processing. We also used additional Notebooks to illustrate how easy it is to implement various machine learning projects with Watson Studio.

In the next chapter, we will provide guidelines for creating a Spark machine learning pipeline within IBM Watson Studio.

6
Using Spark with IBM Watson Studio

In this chapter, we will discuss **Machine Learning (ML)** pipelines and provide guidelines for creating and deploying a Spark machine learning pipeline within IBM Watson Studio.

We will divide this chapter into the following areas:

- Introduction to Apache Spark
- Creating a Spark pipeline in Watson Studio
- Data preparation
- A data analysis and visualization example

Introduction to Apache Spark

Before we get going on creating any kind of a pipeline, we should take a minute to familiarize ourselves with what Spark is and what it offers us.

Spark, built for both speed and ease of use, is a superfast open source engine that was designed with the large-scale processing of data in mind.

Through the advanced **Directed Acyclic Graph** (**DAG**) execution engine that supports **cyclic data flow** and in-memory computing, programs and scripts can run up to 100 times faster than Hadoop MapReduce in memory or 10 times faster on disk.

Spark consists of the following components:

- **Spark Core**: This is the underlying engine of Spark, utilizing the fundamental programming abstraction called **Resilient Distributed Datasets** (**RDDs**). RDDs are small logical chunks of data Spark uses as "object collections".
- **Spark SQL**: This provides a new data abstraction called DataFrames for structured data processing using a distributed SQL query engine. It enables unmodified Hadoop Hive queries to run up to 100x faster on existing deployments and data.
- **MLlib**: This is Spark's built-in library of algorithms for mining big data, common learning algorithms and utilities, including classification, regression, clustering, collaborative filtering, and dimensionality reduction, as well as underlying optimization primitives that best support Spark.
- **Streaming**: This extends Spark's fast scheduling capability to perform real-time analysis on continuous streams of new data.
- **GraphX**: This is the graph processing framework for the analysis of graph structured data.

Watson Studio and Spark

IBM Watson Studio offers certain Spark environments that you can use as default Spark environment definitions to quickly get started with Spark in Watson Studio without having to take the time to create your own Spark environment definitions. This saves setup time and allows you to spend your time creating solutions rather than administering an environment.

Spark environments are available by default for all Watson Studio users. You don't have to provision or associate any external Spark service with your Watson Studio project. You simply select the hardware and software configuration of the Spark runtime service you need to run your tool and then when you start the tool with the environment definition, a runtime instance is created based on your configuration specifications. The Spark compute resources are dedicated to your tool alone and not shared with collaborators—https://medium.com/ibm-watson/ibm-watson-studio-spark-environments-generally-available-f3dda78d3668.

Creating a Spark-enabled notebook

To use Spark in Watson Studio, you need to create a notebook and associate a Spark version with it by performing the following steps:

1. The steps to create the notebook are the same as we have followed in previous chapters. First, from within the project, locate the **Notebook** section and click on **New Notebook**. On the **New notebook** page, provide a name and description:

2. Notice that, in the preceding screenshot, **Python 3.5** is the selected language—this is fine but then if we scroll down, we will see **Spark version***. From the drop-down list, you can select the runtime environment for the notebook. For our example, we can select **Default Spark Python 3.5 XS (Driver with 1 vCPU and 4GB, 2 executors with 1 vCPU and 4 GB RAM each)**:

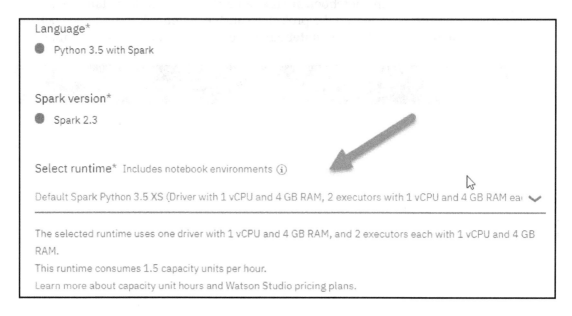

Language*

● Python 3.5 with Spark

Spark version*

● Spark 2.3

Select runtime* Includes notebook environments ⓘ

Default Spark Python 3.5 XS (Driver with 1 vCPU and 4 GB RAM, 2 executors with 1 vCPU and 4 GB RAM ea ⌄

The selected runtime uses one driver with 1 vCPU and 4 GB RAM, and 2 executors each with 1 vCPU and 4 GB RAM.

This runtime consumes 1.5 capacity units per hour.

Learn more about capacity unit hours and Watson Studio pricing plans.

3. Once you click on **Create Notebook**, the notebook environment will be instanced and you will be ready to begin entering Spark commands.

4. Once your Spark-enabled notebook is created, you can run Python commands and execute Spark jobs to process Spark SQL queries using DataFrame abstractions as a data source, as shown in the following example:

```
df_data_2.createOrReplaceTempView("station")
sqlDF = spark.sql("SELECT * FROM station where VALUE > 200")
sqlDF.show()
```

Don't pay too much attention to the actual code in the preceding example at this point as, in the next sections, we will use our Spark-enabled notebook to create a **Spark ML pipeline**.

Creating a Spark pipeline in Watson Studio

So, let's start by understanding just what it is that we mean when we say *pipeline*.

What is a pipeline?

An ML pipeline is characteristically used to **automate** ML workflows, essentially enabling sets of data to be transformed and correlated in a model that can then be tested and evaluated to achieve or estimate an outcome.

Such a workflow consists of four basic areas:

- Data preparation
- Training set generation
- Algorithm training/evaluation/selection
- Deployment/monitoring

Pipeline objectives

A pipeline consists of a sequence of stages. There are two basic types of pipeline stages: **transformer** and **estimator**. As hinted in the *What is a pipeline?* section, a transformer takes a dataset as input and produces an augmented dataset as output, while an estimator abstracts the concept of a learning algorithm and implements a method that accepts data and produces a model.

Even more simply put, a pipeline executes a workflow that can repeatedly prepare new data (for transformation), transform the prepared data, and then train a model (on the prepared data). Another way to summarize is to think of a pipeline as the running of a sequence of algorithms to process and learn from data.

Breaking down a pipeline example

We will start with stepping through the key steps in a Spark pipeline example available within the **IBM Watson Studio Community** (*Use Spark and Python to predict equipment purchase*, submitted by Melanie Manley, July 26, 2018).

In this particular example, we see an existing Spark-enabled notebook that contains steps to load data, create a predictive model, and score data.

The example uses Spark commands to accomplish the tasks of loading data, performing data cleaning and exploration, creating a pipeline, training a model, persisting a model, deploying a model, and scoring a model; however, we will focus here only on the steps that create the Spark ML model. The reader may choose to view the entire example online.

Data preparation

In this step, the data in a DataFrame object is split (using the Spark `randomSplit` command) into three—a **training set** (to be used to train a model), a **testing set** (to be used for model evaluation and testing the assumptions of the model), and a **prediction set** (used for prediction) and then a record count is printed for each set:

```
splitted_data=df_data.randomSplit([0.8,0.18,0.02],24)
train_data=splitted_data[0]
test_data=splitted_data[1]
predict_data=splitted_data[2]
print("Number of training records: " + str(train_data.count()))
print("Number of testing records : " + str(test_data.count()))
print("Number of prediction records : " + str(predict_data.count()))
```

Executing the preceding commands within the notebook is shown in the following screenshot:

```
Number of training records: 48176
Number of testing records : 10860
Number of prediction records : 1216
```

The pipeline

Here, after we have created our three datasets, the Apache Spark ML pipeline will be created, and the model is trained by performing the following steps:

1. First, you need to import the Apache Spark ML packages that will be needed in the subsequent steps:

```
frompyspark.ml.featureimportOneHotEncoder,StringIndexer,IndexToStri
ng,VectorAssembler
frompyspark.ml.classification importRandomForestClassifier
frompyspark.ml.evaluationimportMulticlassClassificationEvaluator
from pyspark.ml import Pipeline, Model
```

2. Next, the example uses the `StringIndexer` function as a transformer to convert all of the string columns into numeric ones:

```
stringIndexer_label=StringIndexer(inputCol="PRODUCT_LINE",outputCol
="label").fit(df_data)
stringIndexer_prof=StringIndexer(inputCol="PROFESSION",outputCol="P
ROFESSION_IX")
stringIndexer_gend=StringIndexer(inputCol="GENDER",outputCol="GENDE
R_IX")
stringIndexer_mar = StringIndexer(inputCol="MARITAL_STATUS",
outputCol="MARITAL_STATUS_IX")
```

3. In the following step, the example creates a feature vector by combining all features together:

```
vectorAssembler_features = VectorAssembler(inputCols=["GENDER_IX",
"AGE", "MARITAL_STATUS_IX", "PROFESSION_IX"], outputCol="features")
```

4. Next, the estimators that you want to use for classification are defined (**random forest** is used):

```
rf = RandomForestClassifier(labelCol="label",
featuresCol="features")
```

5. And finally, convert the indexed labels back into original labels:

```
labelConverter = IndexToString(inputCol="prediction",
outputCol="predictedLabel", labels=stringIndexer_label.labels)
```

6. Now the actual pipeline is built:

```
pipeline_rf = Pipeline(stages=[stringIndexer_label,
stringIndexer_prof, stringIndexer_gend, stringIndexer_mar,
vectorAssembler_features, rf, labelConverter])
```

At this point in the example, you are ready to train the random forest model by using the pipeline and training data you have just built.

A data analysis and visualization example

One of the most exciting advantages of using a Spark-enabled notebook within an IBM Watson Studio project is that all of the data explorations and subsequent visualizations can frequently be accomplished using just a few lines of (interactively written) code. In addition, the notebook interface allows a trial and error approach to running queries and commands, reviewing the results, and perhaps adjusting (the queries) and rerunning until you are satisfied (with the results).

Finally, notebooks and Spark can easily scale to deal with massive (GB and TB) datasets.

In this section, our objective is to use a Spark-enabled notebook to illustrate how certain tasks can be accomplished, such as loading data into the notebook, performing some simple data explorations, running queries (on the data), plotting, and then saving the results.

Setup

Let's take a look at the following sections to understand the setup process.

Getting the data

First things first. We need data. Rather than make some up, we'll follow what several other working examples in the Watson Studio Community have done and download some collected data available publicly from the NOAA **National Climatic Data Center** (**NCDC**): www.ncdc.noaa.gov/data-access/quick-links.

Here's how to get the raw data from the NCDC:

1. From the **National Oceanic and Atmospheric Administration** (**NOAA**) site, click on **Global Historical Climatology Network** (**GHCN**).
2. Click on **GHCN-Daily FTP Access**.

3. Click on the **by_year/** folder.

4. Scroll to the bottom and click on **2015.csv.gz** to download the dataset.

5. After the file has downloaded, extract it to an easily accessible location.

Loading the data

Now we have a file of (although somewhat structured) still raw data. One typical first task when preparing data for analysis is to add column headings. If the file is of reasonable size, you can use a programmer's text editor to open and add a heading row, but if not, you can accomplish this directly in your Spark notebook.

Assuming you've loaded the file into your Watson project (using the process that we have shown in previous chapters), you can then click on **Insert to code** and then select **Insert pandas DataFrame** object as shown in the following screenshot:

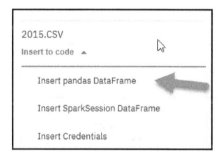

When you click on **Insert pandas DataFrame**, code is generated and added to the notebook for you. The generated code imports any required packages, accesses the data file (with the appropriate credentials), and loads the data into a DataFrame. You can then modify the `pd.read_csv` command (within the code) to include the `names` parameter (as shown in the following code).

This will create a heading row at the top of the file, using the provided column names:

```
df_data_1 = pd.read_csv(body, sep=',',names = ['STATION', 'DATE', 'METRIC',
'VALUE', 'C5', 'C6', 'C7', 'C8'])
```

Running the code in the cell is shown in the following screenshot:

```
File    Edit    View    Insert    Cell    Kernel    Help                                    Trusted | Python 3.5 with Spark  ○

  ⊞    ⊕    ✂  📋  📋    ⬆  ⬇    ▶ Run  ■  C  ⏭    ▦  Format    Code          ▼  📄

  In [1]:
          import types
          import pandas as pd
          from botocore.client import Config
          import ibm_boto3

          def __iter__(self): return 0

          # @hidden_cell
          # The following code accesses a file in your IBM Cloud Object Storage. It includes your credentials.
          # You might want to remove those credentials before you share your notebook.
          client_f20250362df648648ee81858c2a341b5 = ibm_boto3.client(service_name='s3',
              ibm_api_key_id='D2NjbuA02Ra3Pq6OueNW0JZZU6S3MKXOookVfQsKfH3L',
              ibm_auth_endpoint="https://iam.bluemix.net/oidc/token",
              config=Config(signature_version='oauth'),
              endpoint_url='https://s3-api.us-geo.objectstorage.service.networklayer.com')

          body = client_f20250362df648648ee81858c2a341b5.get_object(Bucket='chapter6-donotdelete-pr-qy3imqdyi8jv3w',Key='2015_1.csv')['Body']
          # add missing __iter__ method, so pandas accepts body as file-like object
          if not hasattr(body, "__iter__"): body.__iter__ = types.MethodType( __iter__, body )

          df_data_1 = pd.read_csv(body,names = ['STATION', 'DATE', 'METRIC', 'VALUE', 'C5', 'C6', 'C7', 'C8'])
          df_data_1.head()
```

The raw data in the base file has the format shown in the following screenshot:

```
          Waiting for a Spark session to start...
          Spark Initialization Done! ApplicationId = app-20190214005048-0006
          KERNEL_ID = 27c0d038-9990-481f-a545-0d4cbee627b8

  Out[1]:
```

	STATION	DATE	METRIC	VALUE	C5	C6	C7	C8
0	US1MISW0005	20150101	PRCP	0	T	NaN	N	NaN
1	ASN00015643	20150101	TMAX	373	NaN	NaN	a	NaN
2	ASN00015643	20150101	TMIN	222	NaN	NaN	a	NaN
3	ASN00015643	20150101	PRCP	0	NaN	NaN	a	NaN

Hopefully, you can see that each column contains a weather station identifier, a date, a metric that is collected (such as precipitation, daily maximum and minimum temperatures, temperature at the time of observation, snowfall, snow depth, and so on) and some additional columns (note that missing values may show as **NaN**, meaning *Not a Number*).

Exploration

As we demonstrated in `Chapter 5`, *Machine Learning Workouts on IBM Cloud*, there is plenty of essential functionality common to the `pandas` data structures to support preprocessing and analysis of your data. In this example though, we are going look at examples of data explorations again but this time using Spark DataFrame methods.

For example, earlier we loaded a data file using **Insert pandas DataFrame**; this time, we can reload that file using the same steps, but this time selecting **Insert SparkSession DataFrame**. The code generated will include the `import ibmos2spark` and `from pyspark.sql import SparkSession` commands and load the data into `SparkSession DataFrame` (rather than a `pandas` DataFrame):

```
import ibmos2spark
# @hidden_cell
credentials = {
    'endpoint':
'https://s3-api.us-geo.objectstorage.service.networklayer.com',
    'service_id': 'iam-ServiceId-f9f1f892-3a72-4bdd-9d12-32b5a616dbfa',
    'iam_service_endpoint': 'https://iam.bluemix.net/oidc/token',
    'api_key': 'D2NjbuA02Ra3Pq6OueNW0JZZU6S3MKXOookVfQsKfH3L'
}
configuration_name = 'os_f20250362df648648ee81858c2a341b5_configs'
cos = ibmos2spark.CloudObjectStorage(sc, credentials, configuration_name,
'bluemix_cos')
from pyspark.sql import SparkSession
spark = SparkSession.builder.getOrCreate()
df_data_2 = spark.read\
  .format('org.apache.spark.sql.execution.datasources.csv.CSVFileFormat')\
  .option('header', 'true')\
  .load(cos.url('2015.CSV', 'chapter6-donotdelete-pr-qy3imqdyi8jv3w'))
df_data_2.take(5)
```

Running the cell initiates Spark jobs, shows a progress/status for those jobs, and, eventually, the output generated by the `.take(5)` command:

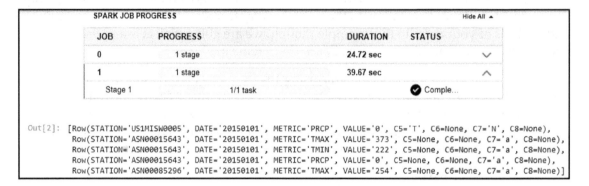

 `SparkSession` is the entry point to Spark SQL. It is one of the very first objects you create while developing a Spark SQL application. As a Spark developer, you create `SparkSession` using the `SparkSession.builder` method (which gives you access to the **Builder API** that you use to configure the session).

Of course, we can also use `count()`, `first` as well as other statements:

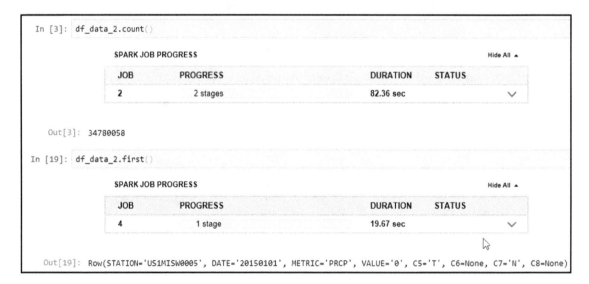

Another interesting and handy analysis method is to show the schema of a DataFrame. You can use the `printSchema()` function to print out the schema for a `SparkR` DataFrame in a tree format, as follows:

```
df_data_2.printSchema()
```

The preceding command yields the following output:

```
root
 |-- STATION: string (nullable = true)
 |-- DATE: string (nullable = true)
 |-- METRIC: string (nullable = true)
 |-- VALUE: string (nullable = true)
 |-- C5: string (nullable = true)
 |-- C6: string (nullable = true)
 |-- C7: string (nullable = true)
 |-- C8: string (nullable = true)
```

A **schema** is the description of the structure of the data. A schema is described using `StructType`, which is a collection of the `StructField` objects (that in turn are tuples of names, types, and nullability classifiers).

Using a Spark DataFrame also provides you with the ability to navigate through the data and apply logic. For example, it's not unreasonable or unexpected to want to look at the first two (or first few) rows of your data by running the `print` command; however, for readability, you might want to add a row of asterisks in between the data rows by using the following code:

```
for row in df_data_2.take(2):
    print(row)
    print( "*" * 104)
```

The preceding code generates the following output:

```
SPARK JOB PROGRESS                                                    Hide All ▲

JOB          PROGRESS                        DURATION      STATUS
8            1 stage                         18.99 sec                    ∨


Row(STATION='US1MISW0005', DATE='20150101', METRIC='PRCP', VALUE='0', C5='T', C6=None, C7='N', C8=None)
********************************************************************************************************
Row(STATION='ASN00015643', DATE='20150101', METRIC='TMAX', VALUE='373', C5=None, C6=None, C7='a', C8=None)
********************************************************************************************************
```

Suppose you are interested in using your SQL skills to perform your analysis?

No problem! You can use **SparkSQL** with your `SparkSession` DataFrame object.

However, all SQL statements must be run against a table, so you need to define a table that acts like a **pointer** to the DataFrame (after you import the `SQLContext` module):

```
from pyspark.sql import SQLContext
sqlContext = SQLContext(sc)
df_data_2.registerTempTable("MyWeather")
```

Additionally, you'll need to define a new DataFrame object to hold the results of your SQL query and put the SQL statement inside the `sqlContext.sql()` method. Let's see how that works.

You can run the following cell to select all columns from the table we just created and then print information about the resulting DataFrame and schema of the data:

```
temp_df =  sqlContext.sql("select * from MyWeather")
print (type(temp_df))
print ("*" * 104)
print (temp_df)
```

This results in the following output:

```
<class 'pyspark.sql.dataframe.DataFrame'>
********************************************************************************************************
DataFrame[STATION: string, DATE: string, METRIC: string, VALUE: string, C5: string, C6: string, C7: string, C8: string]
```

Extraction

Now let's move on to the concept of **extraction**. The print command doesn't really show the data in a very useful format. So, instead of using our Spark DataFrame, we could use the pandas open source data analytics library to create a pandas DataFrame that shows the data in a table.

Now we can look at an example that will make our SQL coders happy.

Import the pandas library and use the .toPandas() method to show the SQL query results:

```
import pandas as pd
sqlContext.sql("select STATION, METRIC from MyWeather limit 2").toPandas()
```

Running the preceding commands results in the following output:

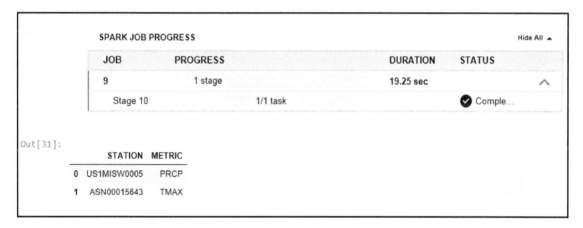

Here is another example of simple SQL query execution, this time counting the number of metrics recorded for each weather station and then creating a list of the weather stations ordered by the number of metric records for the weather station:

```
query = """
select
    STATION ,
    count(*) as metric_count
from MyWeather
group by STATION
order by count(*) desc
"""
sqlContext.sql(query).toPandas()
```

The preceding code gives us the following output:

SPARK JOB PROGRESS				Hide All ▲
JOB	PROGRESS	DURATION	STATUS	
12	2 stages	87.56 sec		∨
13	3 stages	7.46 sec		∨

Out[33]:

	STATION	metric_count
0	USC00218450	8706
1	USC00286055	6204
2	USC00129430	5627
3	USC00116344	5343
4	USW00014607	5325
5	USC00129222	5281
6	USC00172443	5263
7	USW00094860	5131

You are encouraged to experiment with additional variations of SQL statements and then review the results in real time.

Plotting

So, let's move along!

We will now take a look at plotting some of the data we collected in our Spark DataFrame. You can use `matplotlib` and `pandas` to create almost an endless number of visualizations (once you understand your data well enough).

You may even find that, once you reach this point, generating visualizations is quite easy but then you can spend an almost endless amount of time getting them clean and ready to share with others.

We will now look at a simple example of how this process might go.

Starting with the Spark DataFrame from the previous section, suppose that we think that it would be nice to generate a simple bar chart based upon the DATE field within our data. So, to get going, we can use the following code to come up with a count by DATE:

```
df_data_2.groupBy("DATE").count().show()
df_data_2.groupBy("DATE").count().collect()
```

The results of running the preceding code are shown in the following screenshot:

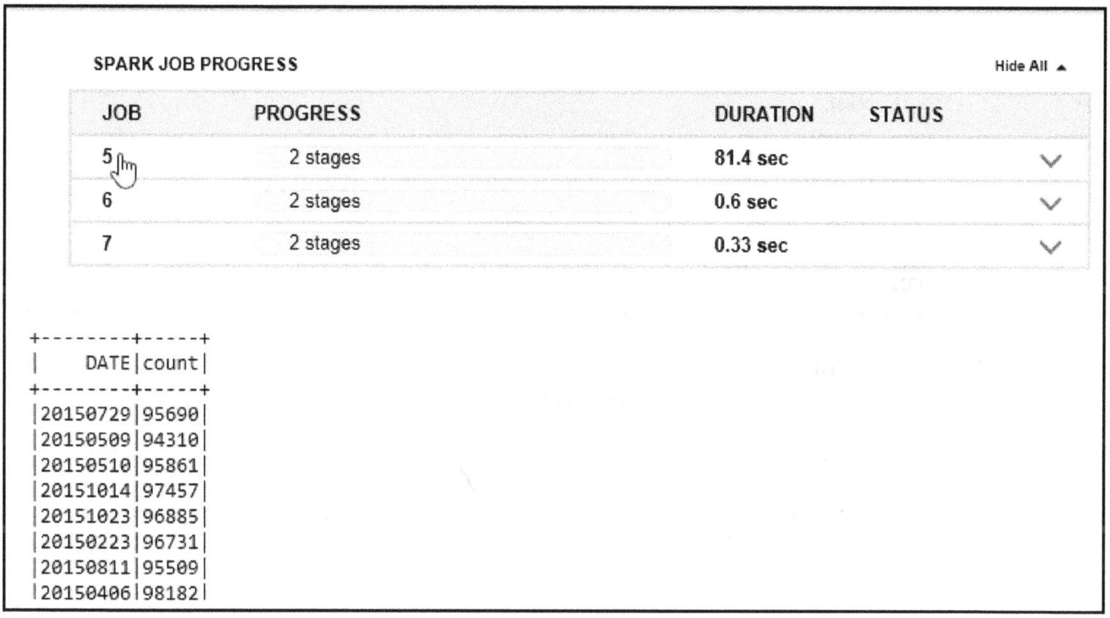

We might say that the output generated seems somewhat reasonable (at least at first glance), so the next step would be to use the following code to construct a matrix of data formatted in a way that can easily be plotted:

```
count = [item[1] for item in df_data_2.groupBy("DATE").count().collect()]
year = [item[0] for item in df_data_2.groupBy("DATE").count().collect()]
number_of_metrics_per_year = {"count":count, "DATE" : year}
import pandas as pd
import matplotlib.pyplot as plt
%matplotlib inline
number_of_metrics_per_year = pd.DataFrame(number_of_metrics_per_year )
number_of_metrics_per_year .head()
```

Running this code and looking at the output generated seems perfectly reasonable and in line with our goal:

SPARK JOB PROGRESS				Hide All ▲
JOB	PROGRESS	DURATION	STATUS	
10	2 stages	80.06 sec		⌄
11	2 stages	77.51 sec		⌄

```
Out[13]:
       DATE   count
0   20150729  95690
1   20150509  94310
2   20150510  95861
3   20151014  97457
4   20151023  96885
```

So, great! If we got to this point, we would think that we are ready to plot and visualize the data, so we can go ahead and use the following code to create a visualization:

```
number_of_metrics_per_year = number_of_metrics_per_year.sort_values(by =
"DATE")
number_of_metrics_per_year.plot(figsize = (20,10), kind = "bar", color =
"red", x = "DATE", y = "count", legend = False)
plt.xlabel("", fontsize = 18)
plt.ylabel("Number of Metrics", fontsize = 18)
plt.title("Number of Metrics Per Date", fontsize = 28)
plt.xticks(size = 18)
plt.yticks(size = 18)
plt.show()
```

After running the preceding code, we can see that the code worked (we have generated a visualization based upon our data) yet the output isn't quite as useful as we might have hoped:

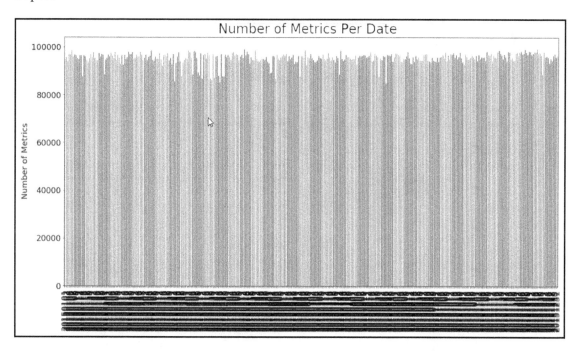

It's pretty messy and not very useful!

So, let's go back and try to reduce the volume of data we are trying to plot. Thankfully, we can reuse some of the code from the previous sections of this chapter.

We can start by again setting up a temporary table that we can query:

```
from pyspark.sql import SQLContext
sqlContext = SQLContext(sc)
df_data_2.registerTempTable("MyWeather")
```

Then, we can create a temporary DataFrame to hold our results (`temp_df`). The query can only load records where `METRIC` collected is `PRCP` and `VALUE` is greater than `500`:

```
temp_df = sqlContext.sql("select * from MyWeather where METRIC = 'PRCP'
and VALUE>500")
print (temp_df)
temp_df.count()
```

This should significantly limit the number of data records to be plotted.

Now we can go back and rerun our codes that we used to create the data matrix to be plotted as well as the actual plotting code but, this time, using the temporary DataFrame:

```
temp_df.groupBy("DATE").count().show()
temp_df.groupBy("DATE").count().collect()
count = [item[1] for item in temp_df.groupBy("DATE").count().collect()]
year = [item[0] for item in temp_df.groupBy("DATE").count().collect()]
number_of_metrics_per_year = {"count":count, "DATE" : year}
import pandas as pd
import matplotlib.pyplot as plt
%matplotlib inline
number_of_metrics_per_year = pd.DataFrame(number_of_metrics_per_year )
number_of_metrics_per_year .head()
number_of_metrics_per_year = number_of_metrics_per_year.sort_values(by =
"DATE")
number_of_metrics_per_year.plot(figsize = (20,10), kind = "bar", color =
"red", x = "DATE", y = "count", legend = False)
plt.xlabel("", fontsize = 18)
plt.ylabel("Number of Metrics", fontsize = 18)
plt.title("Number of Metrics Per Date", fontsize = 28)
plt.xticks(size = 18)
plt.yticks(size = 18)
plt.show()
```

So now we have a different, maybe somewhat better, result but one that is probably still not ready to be shared:

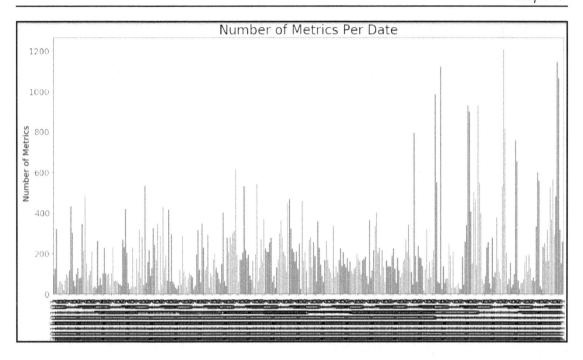

If we continue using the preceding strategy, we could again modify the SQL query to further restrict or filter the data as follows:

```
temp_df =  sqlContext.sql("select * from MyWeather where METRIC = 'PRCP'
and VALUE > 2999")
print (temp_df)
temp_df.count()
```

And then we can review the resulting temporary DataFrame and see that now it has a lot fewer records:

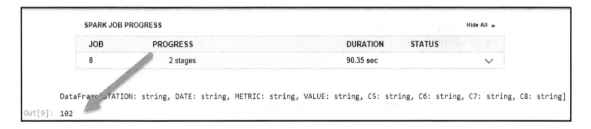

If we now proceed with rerunning the rest of the plotting code, we see that it yields a slightly better (but still not acceptable) plot:

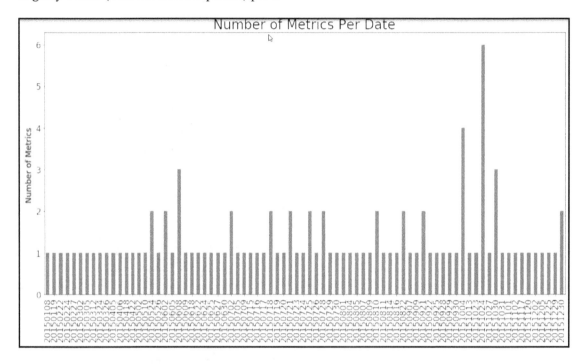

We could, in fact, continue this process of trial and error by modifying the SQL, rerunning the code, and then reviewing the latest results until we are happy with what we see, but you should have the general idea, so we will move on at this point.

Saving

Just like when working in Microsoft Word or Microsoft Excel, it is always a good idea to periodically save your work.

In fact, you may even want to save multiple versions of your work, as you continue to evolve it, in case you want to revert back at some point. While evolving your scripts, you can click on **File**, then **Save** or **Save Version** to keep appropriate copies of your notebook:

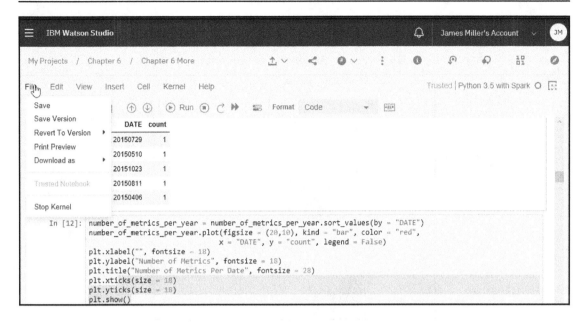

You can also save and share read-only copies of your notebooks *even outside of Watson Studio* so that others who aren't collaborators in your Watson Studio projects can see and download them. You can do this in the following ways:

- **Share a URL on social media**: You can create a URL to share the last saved version of a notebook on social media or with people outside of Watson Studio.
- **Publish on GitHub**: To support collaboration with stakeholders and the data science community at large, you can publish your notebooks in GitHub repositories.
- **Publish as a gist**: All project collaborators who have administrator or editor permission can share notebooks or parts of a notebook as gists. The latest saved version of your notebook is published as a gist.

Downloading your notebook

You can download your notebook as shown in the following screenshot:

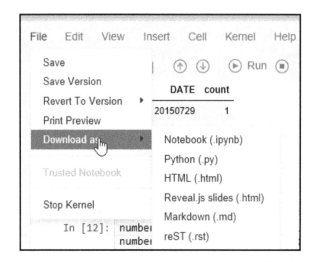

Summary

In this chapter, we introduced both Spark and how to create a Spark-enabled notebook in IBM Watson Studio, as well as the concept of an ML pipeline.

Finally, we finished up with a practical example of using Spark to perform data analysis and create a visualization to tell a better story about the data.

In the next chapter, we will provide an introduction to deep learning and neural networks on IBM Cloud.

7
Deep Learning Using TensorFlow on the IBM Cloud

In this chapter, we will provide an introduction to the concepts of deep learning and neural networks on the IBM Cloud. An overview of how to use the TensorFlow framework to implement deep learning models on the cloud will be provided as well. This chapter is designed to be a balance between theory and practical implementation.

We will cover the following topics in this chapter:

- Introduction to deep learning
- TensorFlow basics
- Neural networks using TensorFlow
- An example
- TensorFlow and image classifications
- Additional preparation

Introduction to deep learning

Deep learning (also known as **deep structured learning** or **hierarchical learning**) is part of a larger group of machine learning approaches based on learning data representations, as opposed to task-specific algorithms.

Learning can be supervised (which we covered in Chapter 3, *Supervised Machine Learning Models and Your Data*), semi-supervised, or unsupervised (covered in Chapter 4, *Implementing Unsupervised Algorithms*).

Deep learning algorithms are at work in exciting areas such as image classification (categorizing every pixels in a digital image into one of several land cover classes, or themes), object detection (the process of finding instances of real-world objects such as faces, cars, and buildings in images or videos), image restoration (to compensate for, or undo, defects caused by motion blur, noise, and camera misfocus, which degrade an image) and image segmentation (the process of partitioning a digital image into multiple segments of pixels, also known as **super-pixels**, to simplify and/or change the representation of an image into something that is more meaningful and easier to analyze).

Deep learning using enormous neural networks is teaching machines to automate the tasks performed by human visual systems.

Deep learning models are vaguely inspired by information processing and communication patterns in biological nervous systems, yet they do differ from the structural and functional properties of biological brains, which make them incompatible with neuroscience evidences.

Enough theory. While the preceding explanation of machine/deep learning may be high-level, it is sufficient enough for us to move on to the next section, where we start thinking about the means of deep learning implementation, specifically using a toolset developed by the Google Brain team for internal Google use, under the Apache 2.0 open source license on November 9, 2015: TensorFlow.

TensorFlow basics

Tensors can be thought to be generalized matrixes or, more specifically, mathematical entities living in structures and interacting with other mathematical entities. If the other entities in the structure are transformed in any way, then the tensor must also be transformed by that transformation rule.

What does the preceding definition mean? Perhaps thinking of a **Tensor** as multidimensional array is easier to grasp, or consider the following, comparing **Scalar**, **Vector**, **Matrix**, and **Tensor**:

$$
\begin{array}{cccc}
\textbf{Scalar} & \textbf{Vector} & \textbf{Matrix} & \textbf{Tensor} \\
1 & \left\{\begin{array}{c} 1 \\ 2 \end{array}\right\} & \left\{\begin{array}{cc} 1 & 2 \\ 3 & 4 \end{array}\right\} & \left\{\begin{array}{cc} \left\{\begin{array}{cc} 1 & 2 \\ 1 & 7 \end{array}\right\} & \left\{\begin{array}{cc} 3 & 2 \\ 5 & 4 \end{array}\right\} \end{array}\right\}
\end{array}
$$

Building on the topic of TensorFlow, TensorFlow is an open source software library (also called a **framework**) originally created by Google for creating deep learning models.

You can visit `https://www.tensorflow.org/` for more details on TensorFlow.

In the next section, we will talk about the connection between deep learning, neural networks, and TensorFlow.

Neural networks and TensorFlow

Deep learning models typically employ algorithms known as **neural networks**, which are said to be inspired by the way actual biological nervous systems (such as the brain) process information. It enables computers to recognize all data points as to what each represents and learn patterns.

Today, the principal software tool for deep learning models is TensorFlow as it permits developers to create large-scale neural networks with numerous layers.

TensorFlow is mainly used for the following purposes:

- Classification
- Perception
- Understanding
- Discovering
- Prediction
- Creation

As noted in the Watson documentation, the challenge with deploying complex machine learning models such as a TensorFlow model is that these models are very computationally expensive and time-consuming to train. Some solutions (to this challenge) include GPU acceleration, distributed computing, or a combination of both. The IBM Cloud platform and Watson Studio offers both of these.

It also points: IBM Watson Studio permits one to leverage the computational power available on the cloud to speed up the training time of the more complex machine learning models, and thus reduce the time from hours or days, down to minutes.

In the next sections, we will explore several exercises demonstrating various ways of using TensorFlow with IBM Watson Studio.

An example

In this section, we will start by stepping through a Watson Community (https://dataplatform.cloud.ibm.com/community) tutorial, designed to demonstrate how easy it is to deploy a deep neural network using the TensorFlow libraries on IBM Watson Studio.

The tutorial is available on GitHub for download, but we won't provide the URL here because we will demonstrate how easy it is to simply import content from external sources (such as GitHub) from directly within a IBM Watson Studio project.

This exercise's key point is that complex machine learning models can be computationally thirsty, but IBM Watson Studio gives you the opportunity to easily and efficiently (pay as you go) use the computational power available on the cloud to speed up processing time and reduce the time it takes to learn from hours, or days, down to minutes.

Additionally, IBM Watson Studio provides all the tools essential to develop a data-centric solution in the cloud. It makes use of Apache Spark clusters (for computational power) and lets you create assets in Python, Scala, and R, and leverage open source frameworks (such as TensorFlow), all of which are already installed on Watson Studio.

If you take the time to read through the details of the tutorial, you will see that it explains how to create a new IBM Cloud account and sign up for IBM Watson Studio (which we already covered in Chapter 1, *Introduction to IBM Cloud*).

The tutorial then goes on to show how to navigate to IBM's Watson Studio (once on the IBM Cloud platform), create a new project, and then import a notebook to the project.

Although, in earlier chapters, we showed how to create a new project in Watson Studio and create new notebooks, this will be the first time we do a notebook import (directly from an external URL), so the next sections will focus on how that process works.

 The notebook that is to be imported will already contain the TensorFlow libraries and example code, so this exercise should be both quick and super easy for us, so let's not waste any more time!

Creating the new project

Taking the same steps that we followed in earlier chapters, we can create a new deep learning IBM Watson Studio project (see the following screenshot) and give it a name:

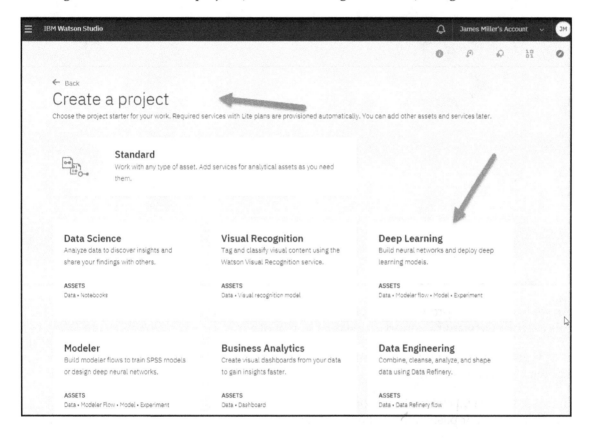

Notebook asset type

Once the new project is created, from the project dashboard, you can click the **Add to project** option and select **Notebook**, as shown in the following screenshot:

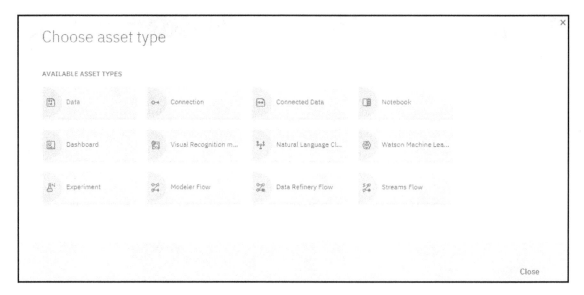

As we have done in preceding chapters, we could create a new, empty notebook. But for this exercise we want to import an existing notebook.

IBM Watson Studio allows you to import notebooks from either a file or directly from a known and accessible URL.

In this case, we will choose to import from a URL. To do that, you select the **From URL** option and type or paste in the following line:

```
https://github.com/aounlutfi/building-first-dl-model/blob/master/first-dl-
model.ipynb
```

The preceding link will be the (external) URL of the notebook to be imported into your Watson Studio project.

Next, click on **Create Notebook** to begin the import (it should only take a few seconds, providing you have access to the URL), as shown in the following screenshot:

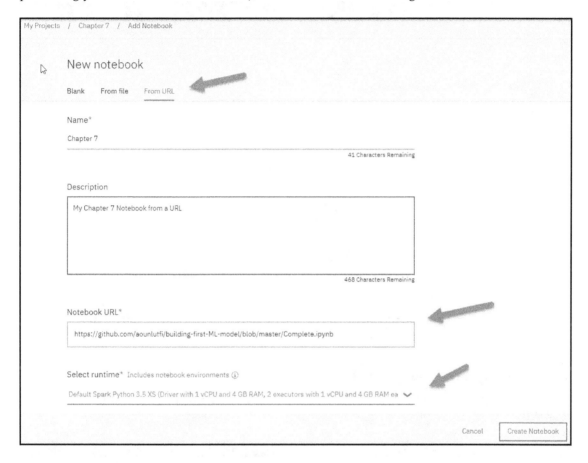

After a few seconds, the notebook opens and is ready for review and execution:

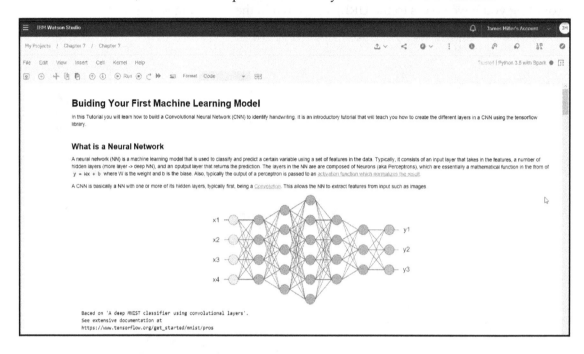

Running the imported notebook

To run the imported notebook, click on **Cell** from the commands ribbon, and then click **Run All**:

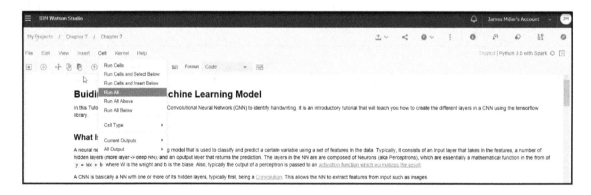

After clicking **Run All**, IBM Watson Studio will then run all the cells within the notebook, which should take (about) fifteen minutes or so to complete, since the data set is made up of 20,000 images.

 You can also run each cell individually, if you want to better understand what is going on.

Reviewing the notebook

If you take the time (and you should) to look through the cells contained in the notebook, you will notice that there are plenty of markdown cells that explicitly describe the steps within the notebook.

For example, you should take note of the markdown cell labeled **Imports** (as shown in the following screenshot) where it clearly states **In order to be able to build, test, and run a NN in TensorFlow, the following imports have to be used. This also imports the MNIST data set (each point in the data set is a handwritten representation of the digits 0-9 in 784 pixels):**

The tutorial also makes a point by challenging you to attempt to set up Python and TensorFlow on a local computer (not on the cloud using IBM Watson Studio) and run the example so that you can compare the results, noting that it may take hours, maybe even days to train, depending on the performance of the machine, and that is after you have assembled the required environment!

In the next example, we will cover using IBM Watson Studio with Watson services and the TensorFlow API to perform image classifications and object detection.

TensorFlow and image classifications

The IBM Watson Visual Recognition service uses deep learning algorithms to identify features like scenes, objects, and faces within images you upload to the service. You can also create and train custom classifiers to identify subjects that meet your requirements, using the Visual Recognition service, IBM Watson Studio, and related Python modules.

To get started with Visual Recognition, we'll need to use the usual procedure to create a Watson Studio project and define a new Python 3.5 Notebook, but we will also need to associate an IBM Watson Visual Recognition service instance with the project (a pretty easy thing to do as it turns out).

Adding the service

To add the Watson Visual Recognition service, you need to go to the IBM Cloud **Dashboard** and select **Watson Services**, then **Browse Services**, where you can then find and select the **Visual Recognition** service:

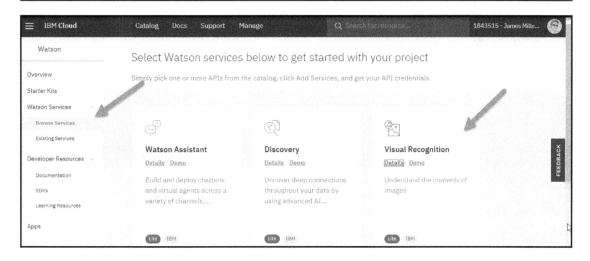

Next, from the **Visual Recognition** page (which is shown in the following screenshot), you can choose a location and resource group for the service instance and then click on **Create** to actually create the instance of the service that you can use in your project:

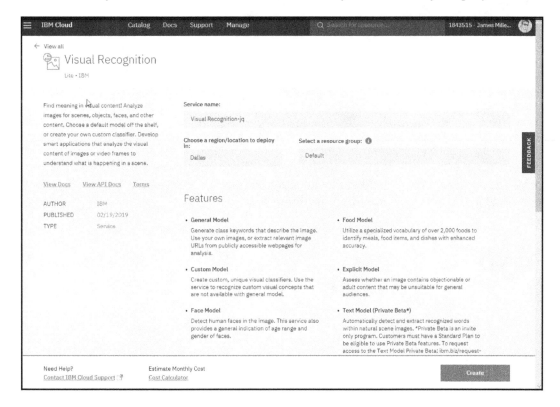

A Visual Recognition service instance may only be associated with one project at a time.

Once you have created the Visual Recognition service instance, it will be listed on your cloud dashboard:

After creating the service instance, you should be able to create what is referred to as **Service Credentials** (or the API key) by clicking on **New Credentials** or **View Credentials** in the **Service credentials** section.

 You will need this API key to refer to and use the instance within the project.

The following screenshot shows the **Service credentials** page:

We will need to refer to this API key in the next few sections of this chapter, so keep it handy!

Now we are ready to get going with the actual Visual Recognition project. In this example (a version is available on GitHub), the Watson Visual Recognition service is used to perform object detection using the TensorFlow object detection API.

Required modules

Although many pre-installed libraries and modules are already included as part of an IBM Watson Notebook environment (depending upon the type of notebook selected), various other modules and frameworks may still need to be installed for a particular project to work correctly, so the first thing we should do in our notebook is to type the following command to see the list of pre-installed libraries:

```
!pip list —isolated
```

It is a very good idea to always begin a new project by using this command to gain an understanding of your notebook's environment; it may save time later.

You can then use the Python `!pip install` command to install each of this project's required modules line by line, as follows:

```
!pip install asn1crypto==0.23.0
!pip install bleach==1.5.0
!pip install certifi==2017.11.5
!pip install cffi==1.11.2
!pip install chardet==3.0.4
!pip install cryptography==2.1.3
!pip install cycler==0.10.0
!pip install enum34==1.1.6
!pip install html5lib==0.9999999
!pip install idna==2.6
!pip install Markdown==2.6.9
!pip install matplotlib==2.1.0
!pip install numpy==1.13.3
!pip install olefile==0.44
!pip install Pillow==4.3.0
!pip install protobuf==3.5.0.post1
!pip install pycparser==2.18
!pip install pyOpenSSL==17.4.0
!pip install pyparsing==2.2.0
!pip install pysolr==3.6.0
!pip install python-dateutil==2.6.1
!pip install pytz==2017.3
!pip install requests==2.18.4
!pip install six==1.11.0
!pip install tensorflow==1.4.0
!pip install tensorflow-tensorboard==0.4.0rc3
!pip install urllib3==1.22
!pip install watson-developer-cloud==1.0.0
!pip install Werkzeug==0.12.2
```

An alternative and more efficient way to install the required modules with one command is to reference the provided `requirements.txt` file:

```
pip3 install -r requirements.txt
```

Using the API key in code

The IBM Watson Visual Recognition service comes with built-in models that you can use to analyze images for scenes, objects, faces, and many other categories without any training. We have already created an instance of the Visual Recognition service, so it is available to our project. For this to work, you need to have that valid key (our actual API key).

Even though you have working Python code in the Watson Notebook, you need to now use your established API key with it, so it will validate with the Watson service (and actually work).

If you look through the Python project code (which we will load in the next section), you will find the following code statement:

```
Visual_recognition = VisualRecognitionV3('2016-05-20', api_key='API_KEY')
```

This line of code is where the Watson Visual Recognition service is initialized as an object we can use within our code. You will replace the API_KEY phrase with your actual API key (the one you created in the previous section).

Additional preparation

In this section, we will take care of a bit more housekeeping that is required before we can successfully run the project.

Pillow is a **Python Imaging Library** (**PIL**), which provides support for opening, manipulating, and saving images. The current version identifies and reads a large number of formats.

This project utilizes `pillow` and requires at least version 5.3.0 to be installed. To ensure that the notebook uses this version, we need to run the following commands:

```
# --- we need pillow version of 5.3.0 to run this project
# --- this code will uninstall the current version:
!pip uninstall -y Pillow
# --- install the 5.3.0 version
!pip install Pillow==5.3.0
# --- import the new one
import PIL
# --- Should print 5.3.0. If it doesn't, then restart the kernel
print(PIL.PILLOW_VERSION)
```

The code uninstalls the currently installed version of Pillow, installs version 5.3.0, imports it into the project, and then prints the (now) currently installed version.

As the final line of code indicates, if the output of the `print` command does not indicate that the `pillow` version installed is 5.3.0, you will need to stop and then restart your kernel (click on **Kernel**, then restart within your notebook), then again execute the `print` command, and you should be ready to go:

```
Uninstalling Pillow-5.3.0:
  Successfully uninstalled Pillow-5.3.0
Collecting Pillow==5.3.0
  Using cached https://files.pythonhosted.org/packages/bc/cc/b6e47b0075ca4267855d77850af7ea4194d2fc591664f1d70e5151b50637/Pillow-5.3.0-cp35-cp
35m-manylinux1_x86_64.whl
Installing collected packages: Pillow
Successfully installed Pillow-5.3.0
5.3.0
```

Upgrading Watson

When I first started experimenting with this project I ran into several difficulties with using the Visual Recognition service. After much debugging and some much appreciated help from IBM Cloud support, it was determined that the project code that I was using was using an older version of the cloud API.

To resolve the issues I was seeing, it was necessary to upgrade the Watson service to the latest version using the following command:

```
# --- Upgrade Watson Developer
!pip install --upgrade "watson-developer-cloud>-2.8.0"
```

The preceding command generates the following output:

```
Collecting watson-developer-cloud>-2.8.0
  Downloading https://files.pythonhosted.org/packages/0b/95/02fae71ded88d5d8ae914773925c2a11986605abf29be3bb6dacd2B8dae7/watson-developer-cloud-2.8.0.tar.gz (283kB)
    100% |████████████████████████████████| 286kB 3.2MB/s eta 0:00:01
Requirement not upgraded as not directly required: requests<3.0,>=2.0 in /opt/conda/envs/DSX-Python35/lib/python3.5/site-packages (from watson-developer-cloud>-2.8.0)
Requirement not upgraded as not directly required: python_dateutil>=2.5.3 in /opt/conda/envs/DSX-Python35/lib/python3.5/site-packages (from watson-developer-cloud>-2.8.
0)
Collecting websocket-client==0.48.0 (from watson-developer-cloud>-2.8.0)
  Downloading https://files.pythonhosted.org/packages/8a/a1/72ef9aa26cfe1a75cee09fc1957e4723add9de098c15719416a1ee85386b/websocket_client-0.48.0-py2.py3-none-any.whl (1
98kB)
    100% |████████████████████████████████| 204kB 4.5MB/s eta 0:00:01
Requirement not upgraded as not directly required: chardet<3.1.0,>=3.0.2 in /opt/conda/envs/DSX-Python35/lib/python3.5/site-packages (from requests<3.0,>=2.0->watson-de
veloper-cloud>-2.8.0)
Requirement not upgraded as not directly required: idna<2.7,>=2.5 in /opt/conda/envs/DSX-Python35/lib/python3.5/site-packages (from requests<3.0,>=2.0->watson-developer
-cloud>-2.8.0)
Requirement not upgraded as not directly required: urllib3<1.23,>=1.21.1 in /opt/conda/envs/DSX-Python35/lib/python3.5/site-packages (from requests<3.0,>=2.0->watson-de
veloper-cloud>-2.8.0)
Requirement not upgraded as not directly required: certifi>=2017.4.17 in /opt/conda/envs/DSX-Python35/lib/python3.5/site-packages (from requests<3.0,>=2.0->watson-devel
oper-cloud>-2.8.0)
Requirement not upgraded as not directly required: six>=1.5 in /opt/conda/envs/DSX-Python35/lib/python3.5/site-packages (from python_dateutil>=2.5.3->watson-developer-c
loud>-2.8.0)
Building wheels for collected packages: watson-developer-cloud
  Running setup.py bdist_wheel for watson-developer-cloud ... done
  Stored in directory: /home/dsxuser/.cache/pip/wheels/c3/24/97/eb1db28970f893acfca84588d4c35d23cfda58d0be3ae8cf08
Successfully built watson-developer-cloud
Installing collected packages: websocket-client, watson-developer-cloud
  Found existing installation: watson-developer-cloud 1.0.0
    Uninstalling watson-developer-cloud-1.0.0:
      Successfully uninstalled watson-developer-cloud-1.0.0
Successfully installed watson-developer-cloud-2.8.0 websocket-client-0.48.0
```

To validate that the service was upgraded, you should see the following message:

```
Successfully installed watson-developer-cloud-2.8.0 websocket-client-0.48.0
```

Once the service was upgraded, all of the issues I was previously experiencing were resolved.

> At the time of writing, 2.8.0 is the latest release. It is advisable to always check for and use the latest available version.

Images

One last setup task to perform is to provide an image file for our solution to detect objects within.

The sample project code offers a picture of four dogs that you can use, but it's more fun to provide one or more of your own. The README notes of this project indicate that the code will expect the file to be located in `test_image/image1.jpg`, but you can simply upload it as a data asset using the same steps we did in previous chapters and then update the code, so it finds the file (you can change the filename as well).

I chose to use the following three different images:

Code examination

At this point, our environment should be ready for the main code section. Let's now look at each section of that code to understand its purpose.

The first section performs various additional imports. Take specific note of the line of code that imports the Visual Recognition service (`VisualRecognitionV3`) from the (now upgraded) `watson_developer_cloud`:

```
from watson_developer_cloud import VisualRecognitionV3
```

The following are the commands:

```
import numpy as np
import os
import six.moves.urllib as urllib
import sys
import tarfile
import tensorflow as tf
import zipfile
import json
from io import StringIO
from PIL import Image
from watson_developer_cloud import VisualRecognitionV3
import matplotlib.pyplot as plt
import matplotlib.patches as patches
```

The next line of code uses our previously mentioned API key (you'll use your own):

```
# --- Replace with your api key
visual_recognition = VisualRecognitionV3('2016-05-20',
api_key='r-1m0OdmBy9khRHJvujylJoLRJIqjwS6Bqwb6VMBfeCE')
```

The next section contains variables that you can experiment with when you run the notebook. Look at the results and adjust the variables to see the effects:

```
MAX_NUMBER_OF_BOXES = 9
MINIMUM_CONFIDENCE = .9
COLORS = ['b', 'g', 'r', 'c', 'm', 'y', 'b', 'w']
```

From the preceding commands, let's explore each of the three variables defined:

- `MAX_NUMBER_OF_BOXES`: This variable represents the maximum number of objects to locate within you test image; I used 9 because it can get ugly if there are a lot of them.

- MINIMUM_CONFIDENCE: This variable represents the minimum confidence score that a box can have. If this value is too low, you may end up with boxes around nothing.
- COLORS: This variable sets the resulting identification boxes' attributes.

Accessing the model

The next sections of the code will download the Visual Recognition model to be used and then load it into memory. Downloading the model may take a few minutes the first time, but it only needs to be downloaded on the first run:

```
# --- define What model to download.
MODEL_NAME = 'ssd_mobilenet_v1_coco_11_06_2017'
MODEL_FILE = MODEL_NAME + '.tar.gz'
DOWNLOAD_BASE = 'http://download.tensorflow.org/models/object_detection/'
# --- Path to frozen detection graph. This is the actual model that  # ---
is used for the object detection.
PATH_TO_CKPT = MODEL_NAME + '/frozen_inference_graph.pb'
print('Downloading model... (This may take over 5 minutes)')
# --- Download model if not already downloaded
if not os.path.exists(PATH_TO_CKPT):
    opener = urllib.request.URLopener()
opener.retrieve(DOWNLOAD_BASE + MODEL_FILE, MODEL_FILE)
 print('Extracting...')
tar_file = tarfile.open(MODEL_FILE)
for file in tar_file.getmembers():
    file_name = os.path.basename(file.name)
if 'frozen_inference_graph.pb' in file_name:
tar_file.extract(file, os.getcwd())
else:
    print('Model already downloaded............')
# --- Load model into memory
print('Loading da model...')
detection_graph = tf.Graph()
with detection_graph.as_default():
    od_graph_def = tf.GraphDef()
    with tf.gfile.GFile(PATH_TO_CKPT, 'rb') as fid:
      serialized_graph = fid.read()
        od_graph_def.ParseFromString(serialized_graph)
      tf.import_graph_def(od_graph_def, name='')
```

Detection

The next part of the code runs the image using the TensorFlow object detection API. It will provide the coordinates of the box as an array of the edge positions (top, left, bottom, and right). It will then crop and save the images based on the boxes. In order for us to crop the correct area we need to transform the coordinates from percentages to pixels by multiplying the values by the width and height:

```
def load_image_into_numpy_array(image):
    (im_width, im_height) = image.size
     return np.array(image.getdata()).reshape(
    (im_height, im_width, 3)).astype(np.uint8)
# --- Path to image to test, was: "test_image/image1.jpg"
TEST_IMAGE_PATH = 'image1.jpg'
```

After we have saved the image portions, we can pass each of them to Watson for classification.

Notice the use of the variables we set previously (MAX_NUMBER_OF_BOXES and MINIMUM_CONFIDENCE) in the following code:

```
print('detecting...')
with detection_graph.as_default():
    with tf.Session(graph=detection_graph) as sess:
        image = Image.open(TEST_IMAGE_PATH)
        image_np = load_image_into_numpy_array(image)
        image_np_expanded = np.expand_dims(image_np, axis=0)
        image_tensor = detection_graph.
        get_tensor_by_name('image_tensor:0')
        boxes = detection_graph.get_tensor_by_name('detection_boxes:0')
        scores = detection_graph.
        get_tensor_by_name('detection_scores:0')
        num_detections = detection_graph.
        get_tensor_by_name('num_detections:0')
        # --- Actual detection.
    (boxes, scores, num_detections) = sess.run([boxes, scores,
num_detections], feed_dict={image_tensor: image_np_expanded})
   # --- Create figure and axes and display the image
        fig, ax = plt.subplots(1)
        ax.imshow(image_np)
        (height, width, x) = image_np.shape
for i in range(0, int(min(num_detections,         MAX_NUMBER_OF_BOXES))):
        score = np.squeeze(scores)[i]
        # --- if the score is not greater than
        # --- what we set the minimun score to be then
        # --- exit the loop
        if score < MINIMUM_CONFIDENCE:
```

```
        break
    box = np.squeeze(boxes)[i]
    box_x = box[1] * width
    box_y = box[0] * height
    box_width = (box[3] - box[1]) * width
    box_height = (box[2] - box[0]) * height
    box_x2 = box[3] * width
    box_y2 = box[2] * height
    img2 = image.crop((box_x, box_y, box_x2, box_y2))
    path = 'cropped/image1'
    os.makedirs(path, exist_ok=True)
    full_path = os.path.join(path, 'img{}.jpg'.format(i))
    img2.save(full_path)
```

Classification and output

Assuming you perform the previously outlined environmental checks and setups outlined earlier in this chapter, all of the code up to this point should run flawlessly without producing any errors. The next section of code was updated from the original version of the project offered on GitHub due to changes IBM made to the newer version of the API.

 If you use the notebook code provided with this book, the updates have already been made for you.

Finally, the next code section receives the results or the classifications back from the Watson Visual Recognition service into an object named `results`.

From that information, a label is then constructed, and a rectangle shape is drawn around each object that was detected within the source image file:

```
# --- Classify images with Watson visual recognition
    with open(full_path, 'rb') as images_file:
        parameters = json.dumps({'threshold': 0.7,
'classifier_ids': ['default']})
        results =
visual_recognition.classify(images_file=images_file,
parameters=parameters).get_result()
        label =
results['images'][0]['classifiers'][0]['classes'][0]['class']
        ax.text(box_x + 5, box_y - 5, label, fontsize=10,
color='white', bbox={'facecolor':COLORS[i % 8], 'edgecolor':'none'})
        # --- Create a Rectangle patch
        rect = patches.Rectangle((box_x, box_y), box_width, box_height,
```

```
        linewidth=2, edgecolor=COLORS[i % 8], facecolor='none')
                ax.add_patch(rect)
```

If you examine the `results` object more closely (try using the Python `type` command on it), you will see that the results object is a Python dictionary object.

 A Python dictionary object is similar to a list in that it is a collection of objects.

Now try adding `print(results)` to the notebook code and you'll get a glimpse of the raw output returned in results.

Using the `print(results)` command, the actual output is shown in the following screenshot:

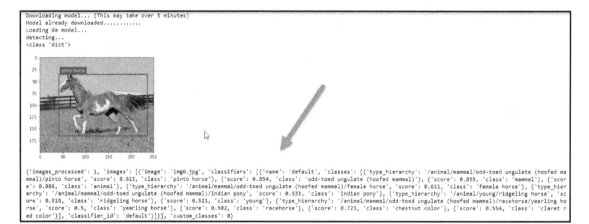

Objects detected

Finally we are ready to use, `matplotlib`, `plt.show()` to display the current image that we are working on:

```
# --- use matplotlib to show the result!
plt.show()
```

We can now finally see the output of the project. In this example, our image was of a horse, and we can see that the Watson Visual Recognition service correctly detected and labeled the object as a pinto horse:

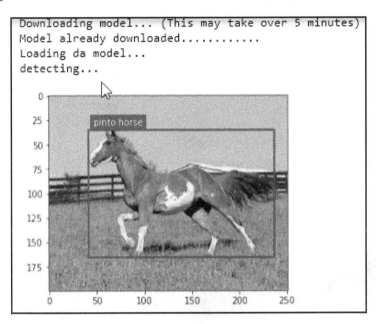

Now the fun part

Now comes the fun part. You can download any number of files from almost anywhere to test the application (or create your own). I used several images and found that Watson was pretty accurate.

The first image used was correctly detected as a motorcycle, the second (an image showing two vintage cars) was close in that Watson detected one of the cars as a car but the other was detected as a light truck.

The results of the final image we already mentioned: Watson not only correctly detected a horse but also labeled its breed: pinto.

The following screenshot shows the three different images and their respective results:

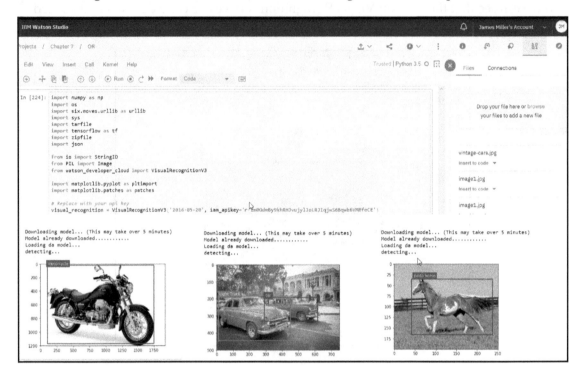

Save and share your work

As always, once you have a working project notebook, you can click on **File** then **Save** to save your work. The next step is to share your notebook by clicking on the **Share** icon, as shown in the following screenshot):

From there, you can select the way you want to share your notebook:

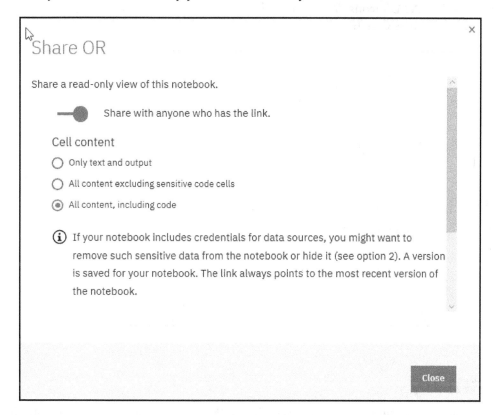

 You should get into the habit of documenting your notebooks with Markdown cell content before sharing it. You will be surprised how much better your work will be received if you add commentary and perspective to each cell.

Finally, when you view your project notebooks (see the following screenshot), note the **SHARED** and **STATUS** icons. You can publish your notebook to various target environments, such as GitHub:

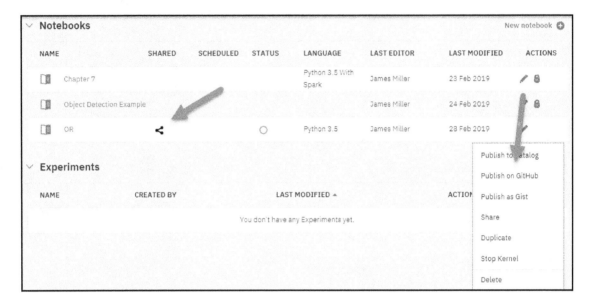

Summary

In this chapter, we started with an introduction to the concepts of deep learning and looked at the basics of using TensorFlow libraries and neural networks.

We then walked through two IBM Watson Studio projects to illustrate how to build both a neural network and an object detection project using the tools and services provided on IBM Cloud.

In the next chapter, we will create a facial expression platform on IBM Cloud.

Section 3: Real-Life Complete Case Studies

3

This part of the book provides complete case studies on how to tackle complete, production-ready machine learning problems from A to Z.

The following chapters will be covered in this section:

- Chapter 8, *Creating a Facial Expression Platform on IBM Cloud*
- Chapter 9, *The Automated Classification of Lithofacies Formation Using ML*
- Chapter 10, *Building a Cloud-Based Multibiometric Identity Authentication Platform*
- Chapter 11, *Conclusion*

8
Creating a Facial Expression Platform on IBM Cloud

In this chapter, we will cover a complete IBM Cloud-based expression classification solution that will use deep learning machine learning techniques on the IBM Cloud platform. The solution will implement a simple, yet efficient, ML model using TensorFlow and the ML services available with IBM Watson Studio. The goal is to illustrate an end-to-end solution for a complex ML task.

We will divide this chapter into the following areas:

- Understanding facial expression classification
- Exploring expression databases
- Preprocessing faces
- Learning the expression classifier
- Evaluating the expression classifier

Understanding facial expression classification

Let's start with a brief discussion leading up to just what we mean when we say *facial expression classification*.

In Chapter 7, *Deep Learning Using TensorFlow on the IBM Cloud*, we used IBM Watson Studio to perform *object detection* within random images. In that use case, we asked our project's model to find or detect common or known objects that might be pictured within an image. For example, we submitted an image of an animal and the solution correctly detected and identified a pinto horse, although no further information about the detected object was produced, such as whether the horse was angry or frightened.

Face detection

Perhaps the next step on this journey (after object detection within an image) is face detection. Face detection is a computer technology being applied in a variety of applications that strive to identify human faces within digital images.

Facial recognition is a way of detecting and identifying a human face through the use of technology. A facial recognition solution utilizes the logic of biometrics to map facial features from a photograph (or even video) and then compares the information with a database of known faces, looking for a match.

 Biometrics is the measurement and statistical examination of people's unique physical and behavioral characteristics, based upon the principle that each and every individual can be accurately identified by his or her intrinsic physical or behavioral traits.

Facial expression analysis

Now we can get to the point: *facial expression analysis*.

This concept commonly classifies all facial expressions as relating to one of the six universal emotions—joy (happiness), surprise, disgust, sadness, anger, and fear as well as neutral.

Emotions are one element that makes us human and (believe it or not) they are difficult to hide, since all emotions, suppressed or not, are likely to have a noticeable physical effect that can be of value if we can automate the process of detecting and then interpreting the physical effects.

Once detected, the interpretation (of facial expressions) process is (perhaps) just another classification exercise. In practice, you'll find that facial expression classification will be based upon what is known as **TBM** or the **transferable belief model** framework.

TBM

TBM offers an interesting premise. Without intending to provide a comprehensive explanation of the TBM framework, a key point is that it introduces degrees of belief and transfer (giving rise to the name of the method: the transferable belief model), which allows the model to make the necessary assumptions required to perform adequate classification (of the expressions). Basically, this means it scores its assumptions, that is, the assumption that the expression is a happy expression is determined to have a n percentage chance of being correct (we'll see this in action later in this chapter when we review the results of our project).

Further (and I'm oversimplifying), TBM looks to use quantified beliefs to make its classification decisions. Something perhaps more easily understood is that facial expression analysis extracts an expression skeleton of facial features (the mouth, eyes and eyebrows) and then derives simple distance coefficients from facial images. These characteristic distances are then fed to a rule-based decision system that relies on TBM in order to assign a facial expression to the face image.

Again, the goal is not to define the theory behind TBM, or even the intimate details of a facial expression analysis solution, but more to show a working example of such; therefore, we will go on to the next section and our use case example and leave to the reader the further work of researching this topic.

Exploring expression databases

At the core of all facial expression analysis solutions is an expression database.

A (**facial**) **expression database** is a collection of images showing the specific facial expressions of a range of emotions. These images must be well annotated or emotion-tagged if they are to be useful to expression recognition systems and their related algorithms.

A major hindrance to new developments in the area of **automatic human behavior analysis** is the lack of suitable databases with displays of behavior and affect. There have been directed advances in this area, as in the **MMI Facial Expression Database** project, which aims to deliver large volumes of **visual data of facial expressions** to the facial expression analysis community.

The MMI Facial Expression Database was initially created in 2002 as a resource for building and evaluating facial expression recognition algorithms. One significance of this database is that others databases focus on the expressions of the six basic emotions (which we mentioned earlier), whereas this database contains both these prototypical expressions as well as expressions with a single **Facial Action Coding System** (**FACS**) or **Action Unit** (**AU**) activated, for all existing AUs and many other **Action Descriptors** (**AD**). Recently recordings of naturalistic expressions have been added too.

The database is freely available to the scientific community. Find out more about the database online at `https://mmifacedb.eu`.

In other example projects, we've been able to create our own test data or alter existing datasets to use within a project. However, with **expression analysis** projects, it is really not realistic to create a reasonably sized database (stating with nothing), which would require the collection and processing of literally thousands of images, all appropriately documented.

After collection, each (facial) image needs to be reviewed and categorized based on the emotion shown into one of seven categories (angry, disgust, fear, happy, sad, surprise, and neutral). To further complicate this work, images may not be aligned and properly proportioned.

The bottom line is that, even if you have a large number of images, if the images are not correctly labeled or simply do not contain detectable facial images, the performance of the expression analysis and detection process will be compromised (it will perform poorly).

These types of challenges make the classification process more difficult because the model is forced to generalize.

Training with the Watson Visual Recognition service

Considering the above mentioned challenges, IBM Watson Studio helps us to get started anyway by offering (right out of the box) the **Watson Visual Recognition** service.

This valuable service helps with the process of accurately analyzing, classifying, and training images using machine learning logic (although, to be sure, it still requires reasonable amounts of relevant training data to begin with, but more on that in a bit).

Thankfully, there is a set of built-in models that is available to us to provide highly accurate results without endless training. The models are as follows:

- **General model**: General classifier categories
- **Face model:** Locate faces within an image, gender, and age
- **Explicit model**: Whether an image is inappropriate for general use
- **b model**: Specifically for images of food items

In this chapter's project, we will show how to use the Visual Recognition Service and the Face model to build an end-to-end working solution that can look at an image of a human face, perform expression analysis and simple classification, and ultimately, determine whether the individual is feeling happy or sad.

Preprocessing faces

We have just mentioned that building a suitable expression database is a lot of work. To be able to build an end-to-end working expression analysis solution (and fit it all into a single chapter of this book), we will take some liberties with our project:

- We will limit our model's ability to detect and classify only two emotions—happiness and sadness
- We will supply only a limited amount of expression data to train our model

Obviously, in the real world, our second assumption is a risky one; as in any ML model, less training data typically produces a less valuable result.

Preparing the training data

Again, if we have decided to satisfy only the minimal requirements for using the face model and the Visual Recognition service, we can get away with collecting only 10 images for each class which we intend our model to train on (10 happy faces, 10 sad faces, and 10 negative faces).

These individual training files will need to be the following:

- Either JPEG (`.jpg`) and PNG (`.png`) formatted
- At least 32*32 pixels in size
- Compressed as a group into class ZIP files, that is, 10 happy faces in a `happy.zip` file and 10 sad faces in a `sad.zip` file

A sampling of our initial happy model training data is shown in the following screenshot:

The preceding images are of 10 faces showing what we think can be labeled as being representative of happy facial expressions. Notice that the individual files have all been added to a compressed (ZIP) file named `happy.zip`.

A sampling of our initial sad model training data is shown in the following screenshot:

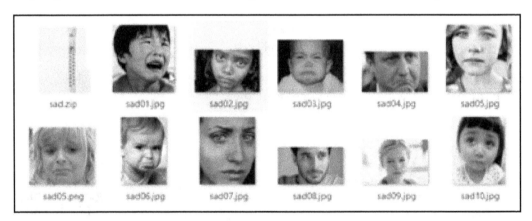

And clearly, as the former group displayed happiness, the later images are of faces showing what we think can be labeled as being representative of sad expressions (individual files and the zipped file, `sad.zip`).

Negative or non-positive classing

For the face model to work correctly, negative images are also required, not to be used to create a class (we will cover this in an upcoming section) within the created classifier, but to define what the updated classifier is not. Negative example files should not contain images that have the subject of any of the positive classes (happy and sad). In essence, the face images in this group should be perhaps considered to be neutral. You only need to specify one negative example file.

> Because you want to give the model examples of what not to look for, you must provide the negative class. Providing a ML model with all positive images would mean that it would just assume that everything is positive and produce a risky result.

So finally, our initial negative model training data is shown in the following screenshot:

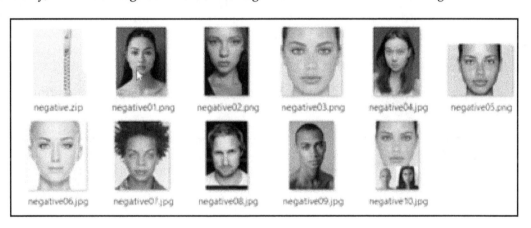

Preparing the environment

Let's now get moving along with the project model development.

The next step (assuming you have already created a new IBM Watson Studio project) is to associate the Watson Visual Recognition Service to the project. We covered how to do this in Chapter 7, *Deep Learning Using TensorFlow on the IBM Cloud*, so we will assume you have already added the service to this new project. If not, review Chapter 7, *Deep Learning Using TensorFlow on the IBM Cloud*, or the online Watson Studio documentation.

Project assets

In this chapter's project, our assets will primarily be the training images we have collected and, indirectly perhaps, classified. These image assets are added in a way similar to the process we used to add data assets to Watson Studio projects in earlier chapters, but there are a few differences, which we will soon see.

For now, we will perform the following steps:

1. Go to the **Assets** tab and, under **Models**, click on **New Visual Recognition model**:

2. Once the model is created (it should take only a few moments), you can browse to or drag and drop the training (.zip) files we collected in the earlier section of this chapter to add them to our new project. This will upload the image files to **Cloud Object Storage (COO)**, making them available to be used in our project:

You do not have to load each image file independently, just the three zipped files (`happy.zip`, `sad.zip`, and `negative.zip`). The ZIP files should then be listed as shown in the preceding screenshot.

Although you can upload the ZIP files, Watson will not allow those ZIP files to use the Preview feature on the **Data Assets** page. This is not a problem though, as you can still preview the images from the **Model** page, as we will see shortly.

Creating classes for our model

Now, from the **Default Custom Model** page, we need to create two classes. Perform the following steps to create the class for the model:

1. Click on **Create a class.**
2. Enter a class name for it.

3. Click the blue **Create** button:

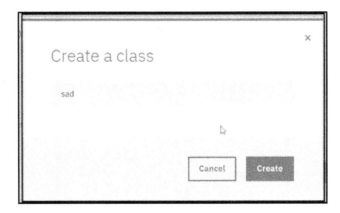

We actually only need to create two classes for this project: happy and sad, since Watson has already created the negative class for us. There is only one negative class per model, but you can have as many other classes as required for your project's objectives.

Once the classes are created, you then need to simply drag and drop the .zip files into the corresponding classes as shown in the following screenshot:

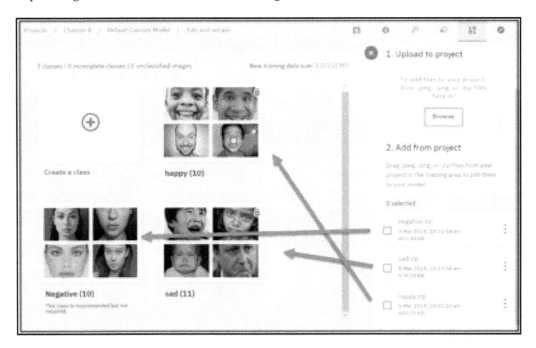

As you can see, we dropped each of the three ZIP files onto their corresponding class panes.

As we stated earlier in this chapter, Watson preview doesn't work with zipped image file assets; however, from the **Default Custom Model** page (shown in the following screenshot) we can click on **All Images** and scroll through what was loaded to see the filename, label, and content:

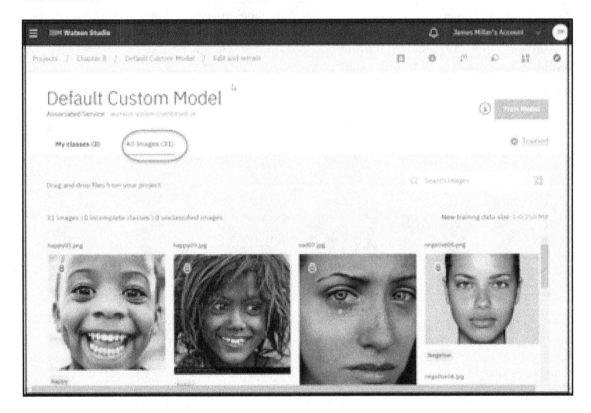

Automatic labeling

Earlier in this chapter, we pointed out that, after collecting images to be used for expression analysis and recognition, each individual image must be annotated or labelled as to which emotion group it belongs to. This can be a daunting task. Fortunately, when using IBM Watson Studio, you can simply include the appropriate images in a ZIP file and drop the ZIP file onto a class and Watson will automatically label the image file. For example, in the following screenshot, you can see that we can correctly identify those images to include within our **happy** class (shown outlined in green) while a single image, sad05 (shown outlined in red), does not belong to and should be excluded from our ZIP file:

This is a pretty easy process, but it could invite errors. Since it is easy and quick, you may mistakenly include images that will dilute the training sample. Keep in mind that, even if the image files are named intuitively, such as happy or sad, Watson doesn't care about the names, it simply labels all of the images in the file as *positive* or *matching* to the class.

Finally, there's one more note about the training data. Once you go to the trouble of collecting and uploading data as an IBM Watson Studio asset, that data is available to any of your projects and, if you want to, you can share it with any other Watson Studio user! This promotes the development of assets across projects and users and increases the return on your investment.

Learning the expression classifier

Once you notice that the model status (indicated at the upper-right of the **Default Custom Model** page) has changed to **Model is ready to train**, you can then click on the **Train Model** button to start training the Face model on the training images we provided:

Since we provided only roughly 30 training images, the training process should take less than 5 or 10 minutes. During the training, you will not be able to make any changes to the model or classes.

Evaluating the expression classifier

Once the model training is complete, you should see the following **Training successful** message:

From this point, you can click on the **here** hyperlink in the popup to view and test the model.

Viewing the model training results

After successfully training the model, you will be redirected to a page where you can see an overview or **Summary** (**Model ID**, **Status**, and other metadata) of the model build (take a note of the **Model ID** as that will be required during the implementation stage):

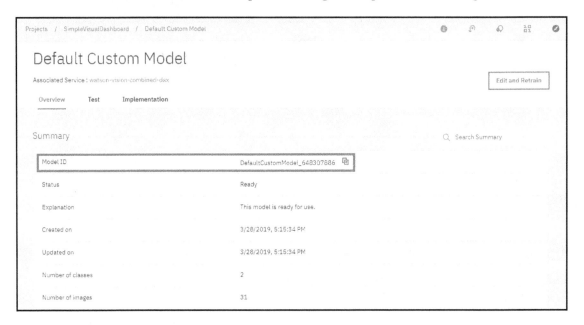

We can also see our model's **Classes** information:

Testing the model

To test and understand how our model performs (or whether it even works!), you can upload images in the **Test** tab of the previous page view. Let's try it!

To test with images, click on **Test**:

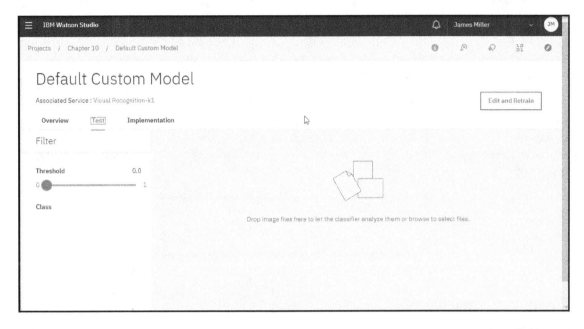

Like we did to collect our happy and sad images, we can identify several random images (without regard to the expression shown in the image) to test our models ability to detect expression:

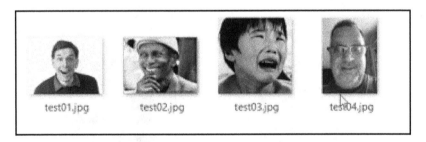

Test scores

The idea is for our model to interpret the preceding images, perform some expression analysis, and then classify each image as either happy or sad facial expressions. In addition, the model should generate and display a score for each of the defined classes (except for the negative class).

As you have seen in our model, we defined just two classes to be classified—happy and sad. The model should, for each test image, display a percentage score showing the percentage of whether the detected expression is happy or sad. For example, the following score indicates that there is approximately 90 percent chance that the expression identified is happy:

Test the model

To test the model with the following images, we can simply drag and drop the image files onto the preceding page to let the classifier analyze them:

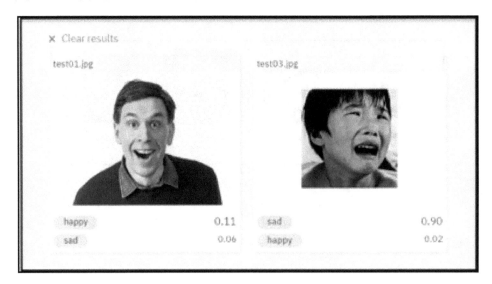

Take a look at the following screenshot as well:

Success! It appears that all four of our random faces have been evaluated and scored by our Face model correctly. We can see that, in the first two images, the model indicates 11 and 90 percent that the individuals are happy and sad, respectively.

Improving the model

Even though it appears that our little solution is working correctly, we still have to keep in mind that the model has been trained on a very small amount of data.

To improve the model, from the **Default Custom Model** page, you can click on the blue button labeled **Edit and Retrain**:

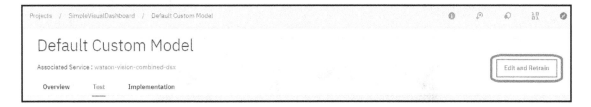

This will make our project editable.

More training data

Some improvements to our solution would include adding additional images to the happy and sad groups. To do this, you can create a new ZIP file with new and additional images and upload it to IBM Watson Studio (in the same fashion as we did earlier in this chapter), upload the file, and drop the new ZIP file into the respective class. Watson will add the new images (and not overwrite what's already been defined):

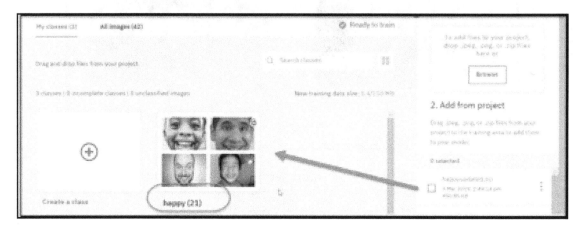

Adding more classes

Another great improvement for our solution would be to add additional classes. This is to allow our model to support the detection of, perhaps, a third emotion or expression other than happy and sad. Let's try to add anger as our third (not counting negative) class:

1. The first step, of course, is to collect and compress (zip up) our angry images training data:

Remember that it is not important what the individual image files are named, but it is important that they all represent the same emotion, *anger*.

2. After we upload the `angry.zip` file (as another data asset available to our project), we can then go ahead and click on **Create a class**, enter `angry` for the class name, and then click on **Create**:

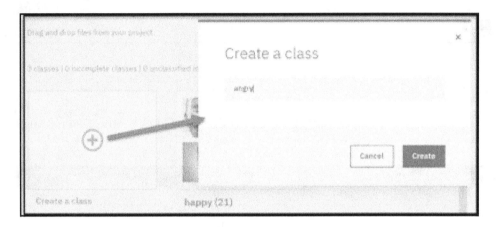

After a moment or two, our new `angry` class is ready:

3. Now we can once more click on the **Train Model** button to start retraining the Face model on the training images we provided, along with our new angry class. After a few moments, we should see the **Model Trained** message again:

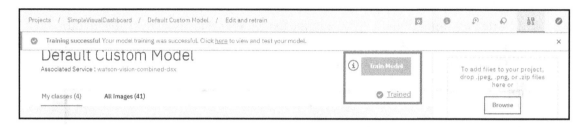

Results

Once again, we can go to the **Default Custom Model** page, click on the **Test** tab, and drop some new test images for the model to evaluate and classify:

You can see that the model has correctly classified the first image as 0.77 angry. We also retested a previous image as a bit of a regression test and the model again correctly classified it (as 0.66 happy).

Notice that now our model provides three scores for each test image: **angry**, **happy**, and **sad**, corresponding to each of our model's defined classes:

Summary

In this chapter, we explored the concepts behind expression analysis and detection and used IBM Watson Studio, the Watson Visual Recognition service, and the default face model to build, train, and test an end-to-end, working visual expression classification solution with almost zero programming!

In the next chapter, we will discover automated classification of lithofacies formation using ML on the IBM Cloud platform.

9
The Automated Classification of Lithofacies Formation Using ML

In this chapter, we will explore the idea of building an end-to-end cloud-based machine learning system to identify **lithofacies** based on well log measurements. This is a crucial step in all drilling applications. First, we will start by introducing the problem and the dataset. Next, we will explain the types of preprocessing and post processing needed for such a use case. Finally, a complete solution will be built using machine learning services, Python, and IBM Watson Studio.

The following topics will be covered in this chapter:

- Understanding lithofacies
- Exploring the data
- Training the classifier
- Evaluating the classifier

Understanding lithofacies

Sedimentary rock that has been formed through the deposition and solidification of sediment transported by water, ice, and wind is usually deposited in layers. The geological properties of these layers depend upon a number of forces such as tectonics, sea level, sediment supply, physical and biological processes of sediment transport and deposition, and climate. The result of these forces and interactions yield what is known as a **geometric arrangement**, making up the stratigraphic architecture of an area. The arrangement or internal anatomy of the sediment bodies within the architecture is identified through lithofacies analysis and the interpretation of the depositional environments.

Gathering and interpreting this information is a critical component in the work of oil and gas, groundwater, and mineral and geothermal exploration (as well as being a significant share of environmental and geotechnical study).

Depositional environments

The previously mentioned depositional environments are created by the various physical and biological processes of transporting and depositing sediments. These processes result in various distributions of grain size and biogenic sedimentary structures that characterize (or classify) the deposited sediment through a direct relationship to the depositional force that produced them.

Relating the features found in an environmental structure back to the forces that created them is the basic method used by geologists to interpret the depositional environment of the sedimentary sequence.

Lithofacies formation

One of the very first steps in the progression of **lithofacies analysis** (and, therefore, lithofacies formation), is the description and interpretation of available and conventional core data.

An important outcome of core describing is the subdivision of cores into lithofacies, defined as **classifications of a sedimentary sequence** based on lithology (the study of the characteristics of rock), grain size, physical and biogenic sedimentary structures, and the stratification that relates to the depositional processes that produced them.

Lithofacies and lithofacies associations (groups of related lithofacies) are the basic units for the interpretation of depositional environments.

Our use case

I hope that after reading the preceding sections of this chapter, you have already formulated the idea that a critical component in evaluating opportunities for drilling applications is lithology and lithofacies formation.

Our goal, in this project, is to use machine learning to interpret core data and identify lithofacies (that is, classify bodies of rock or rock types into mappable units of a designated stratigraphic unit) based upon its physical characteristics, composition, formation, or various other attributes, obtained in well logging data.

Exploring the data

In the following sections, we will explore the well training data and plot the learning in various forms.

Well logging

Well logging, sometimes referred to as **borehole logging,** is the practice of making a detailed record (or a well log) of the geological formations penetrated by a borehole or a well. This log may be established either on a visual inspection of the samples brought to the surface (called **geological logs**) or on the physical measurements made by instruments lowered into the hole (called geophysical logs).

Geophysical well logs such as, drilling, completing, producing, or abandoning can be done during any phase of a well's history.

Log ASCII Standard (LAS)

Thankfully, there is a commonly acceptable format in which well logs are expected to be.

LAS is an industry-standard file format used in all oil-and-gas and water well industries to log and store well log information and data. A single LAS file can only contain data for one well. But in that one well, it can contain any number of datasets (called **curves**). Common curves found in an LAS file may include natural gamma, travel time, resistivity logs, and other possible information.

 For more information on LAS files, you can refer to this paper: `https://www.bcogc.ca/node/11400/download`.

Wow! Although not rocket science, the data is not a simple relational table. Preliminary work for this exercise will be to better understand the specifics of the data provided.

In this chapter, our goal is to implement a machine learning algorithm in Python using `scikit-learn`, one of the most popular machine learning tools for Python, based upon a sample well drilling log dataset for the task of training a classifier to distinguish between different types of lithofacies.

Suppose that we are told that the training log dataset was created from sample logs, and based upon research defining eight different lithofacies, along with various log measurements, such as gamma-ray, neutron porosity, **photoelectric factor** (**PeF**), and resistivity.

We also know that in this file, we'll have six lithofacies data points (`GCR`, `NPHI`, `PE`, `PEF`, `ILD`, and `ILM`), along with an ID and the lithofacies type.

The following screenshot shows a portion of the top section of an actual well logging file:

```
# 10/30/2000 11:16:43 Updated by the Kansas Geological Survey
# #KGS#ID: 01S02E/1020069094
# #KGS#INPUT_FILE: /home/crude2_3/WellLogs/Doveton-Dakota_2000_10_30/gaydusek.las.las
~VERSION INFORMATION
 VERS              .                    2.0: CWLS log ASCII Standard -VERSION 2.0
 WRAP              .                     NO: One line per depth step
~WELL INFORMATION
#MNEM.UNIT              DATA        DESCRIPTION OF MNEMONIC
#---------     -------------   -------------------------------
 STRT          .F                 50.5000: Start Depth                      I
 STOP          .F                525.0000: Stop Depth
 STEP          .F                  0.5000: Step Length
 NULL          .                -999.0000: Null Value
 COMP          .     KANSAS GEOLOGICAL SURVEY: Company
 WELL          .              GAYDUSEK W II: Well
 FLD           .                    WILDCAT: Field
 LOC           .                   10-1S-2E: Location
 LOC1          .                   NW SW NW: Location Line 1
 COUN          .                 WASHINGTON: County
 STAT          .                     KANSAS: State
 CTRY          .                        USA: Country
```

The following screenshot is a peek at a portion of our file, which we will use for training our machine learning model. This file excludes the top LAS-formatted section headers and is simply a continuous list of curves or well-logging measurements:

```
WellTraining.csv - Notepad
File  Edit  Format  View  Help
lito_ID,lithofacies,GCR,NPHI,PE,PEF,ILD,ILM
1,Pkst/Pkst-Grnst,8,1.812,-2.309,1.116,3.187,5.615
2,Sucrosic (Dol),36,1.658,6.496,10.585,6.404,12.543
3,Pkst/Pkst-Grnst,5,5.530,3.265,0.078,6.514,1.917
4,NM Silt & Sand,4,-0.683,8.798,3.019,-5.334,14.279
5,Mar Shale & Silt,102,3.489,7.608,5.129,4.809,-1.541
6,Mdst/Mdst-Wkst,66,6.706,9.689,4.523,11.142,6.391
7,Grnst/PA Baff,46,-2.399,7.458,,1.291,-9.354
8,Nm ShlySilt,76,9.998,8.480,18.371,5.031,0.199
9,Sucrosic (Dol),72,2.802,3.380,0.293,2.717,7.569
10,Grnst/PA Baff,10,3.573,-9.874,,6.743,-5.429
11,Nm ShlySilt,37,10.407,12.152,1.765,13.020,9.599
12,Mdst/Mdst-Wkst,55,3.586,-0.249,7.089,-0.929,7.472
```

Loading the data asset

We will assume that you have created a new IBM Watson Studio project, and therefore, you can proceed to add a data asset (our well sample log file) to it so that we can work with the data. We have loaded data files in our previous chapters, but here is a quick refresher:

1. From the new project's **Assets** page, click on **Add to project | DATA**
2. In the **Load** pane that opens, browse to the file. Remember that you must stay on the page until the load is complete
3. IBM Watson then saves the files in the object storage that is associated with your project, and they are listed as data assets on the **Assets** page of your project

Data asset annotations

As you build your assets within IBM Watson Studio, it is highly recommended that you take the time to annotate your data assets at the time that you load them. This will allow you to quickly search for and locate those assets for collaboration with others and to use within other projects. You can accomplish this by simply adding a description and one or more tags to your asset.

A tag is metadata that simplifies searching for your assets. A tag consists of one string containing spaces, letters, numbers, underscores, dashes, and the # and @ symbols. You can create multiple tags on the same asset by using a comma to separate the individual tag values.

From the project page, under **Data assets**, you can click on the asset name:

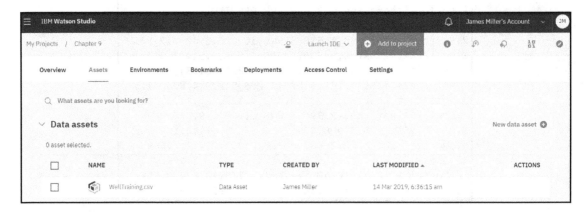

Next, click inside the **Tags** box to add tags, and you can manually assign business terms and tags to the data, as well as a description, as shown in the following screenshot:

Profiling the data

Another method for developing a good understanding of what your data offers is to create a profile of the data, using the profile feature within IBM Watson Studio.

The profile of a data asset includes generated metadata and statistics about the textual content of the data so that you can *see* how it is made up. You can create a profile on the asset's **Profile** page in the project, as shown in the following screenshot:

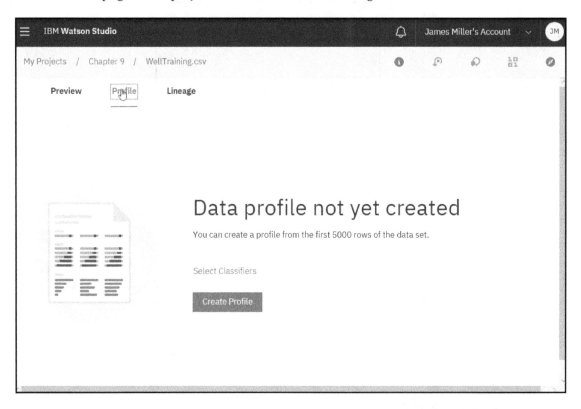

Once you click on **Create Profile**, IBM Watson reviews the data and generates the visuals that you can scroll though and easily examine:

 Depending upon the size and complexity of the data, generating the profile may take a few minutes. The good news is that after it is created, it is saved with the file so that it doesn't have to be generated again.

Using a notebook and Python instead

Rather than using the profiler, you can use visualizations within an IBM Watson notebook to present data visually to identify patterns, gain insights, and make decisions based upon your project's objectives or assumptions. As we've seen in earlier chapters, many open source visualization libraries, such as `matplotlib`, are already pre-installed on IBM Watson Studio for you, and all you have to do is import them.

 You can install other third-party and open source visualization libraries and packages in the same manner, or take advantage of other IBM visualization libraries and tools, such as **Brunel**, to create interactive graphs with simple code and SPSS models to create interactive tables and charts to help evaluate and improve a predictive analytics model.

In the next few sections, we will use a notebook and Python commands to show the various ways to analyze and condition data.

Loading the data

Again, since we assume that we already have a new IBM Watson Studio project created, we can go ahead and add a new notebook to the project (from your project, click on **Add to Project | Notebook**, just as we did in prior chapters, just be sure to specify the language as Python). Let's take a look at the following steps:

1. Load and open the file, then print the first five records (from the file). Recall that to accomplish this, there is no coding required.

2. You simply click on **Insert to code** and then **Insert pandas DataFrame** for our file in the **Files | Data Asset** pane:

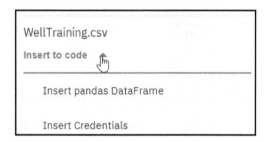

This automatically generates the following code in our notebook's first cell, which will load our data file into a pandas DataFrame object (df_data_1) and then print the first five records of the file:

```
In [78]:  import types
          import pandas as pd
          from botocore.client import Config
          import ibm_boto3

          def __iter__(self): return 0

          # @hidden_cell
          # The following code accesses a file in your IBM Cloud Object Storage. It includes your credentials.
          # You might want to remove those credentials before you share your notebook.
          client_f20250362df648648ee81858c2a341b5 = ibm_boto3.client(service_name='s3',
              ibm_api_key_id='WpjIPTTCLB8aR9oMzbL1ZOs1t0q2PtRpYy3SLD4cjcT6',
              ibm_auth_endpoint="https://iam.bluemix.net/oidc/token",
              config=Config(signature_version='oauth'),
              endpoint_url='https://s3-api.us-geo.objectstorage.service.networklayer.com')

          body = client_f20250362df648648ee81858c2a341b5.get_object(Bucket='chapter9-donotdelete-pr-oef5e5dul7dtej',K
          # add missing __iter__ method, so pandas accepts body as file-like object
          if not hasattr(body, "__iter__"): body.__iter__ = types.MethodType( __iter__, body )

          df_data_1 = pd.read_csv(body)
          df_data_1.head()
```

The preceding code generates the following output for us:

Out[78]:

	lito_ID	lithofacies	GCR	NPHI	PE	PEF	ILD	ILM
0	1	Pkst/Pkst-Grnst	8	1.812	-2.309	1.116	3.187	5.615
1	2	Sucrosic (Dol)	36	1.658	6.496	10.585	6.404	12.543
2	3	Pkst/Pkst-Grnst	5	5.530	3.265	0.078	6.514	1.917
3	4	NM Silt & Sand	4	-0.683	8.798	3.019	-5.334	14.279
4	5	Mar Shale & Silt	102	3.489	7.608	5.129	4.809	-1.541

From this review, we can see that each row of the dataset represents one lithofacies, and they are each represented by several features that are in our table's columns (as shown in the preceding screenshot).

Using the `print` and `.shape` functions of Python, we see that we have 180 lithofacies (the number of records in the file) and 8 features in the dataset:

```
In [79]: print(df_data_1.shape)
                (180, 8)
```

3. We can also use the `.unique()` function to demonstrate that we have eight different types of lithofacies in our dataset:

```
In [80]: print(df_data_1['lithofacies'].unique())
            ['Pkst/Pkst-Grnst' 'Sucrosic (Dol)' 'NM Silt & Sand' 'Mar Shale & Silt'
             'Mdst/Mdst-Wkst' 'Grnst/PA Baff' 'Nm ShlySilt' 'Wkst/Wkst-Pkst']
```

4. Next, we can use the `.size()` function to see how each lithofacies is represented within the file. The data seems pretty balanced between `22` and `25`, with the `Mdst/Mdst-Wkst` lithofacies being the most unbalanced with `16`:

```
In [81]:  print(df_data_1.groupby('lithofacies').size())

          lithofacies
          Grnst/PA Baff      22
          Mar Shale & Silt   23
          Mdst/Mdst-Wkst     16
          NM Silt & Sand     22
          Nm ShlySilt        26
          Pkst/Pkst-Grnst    23
          Sucrosic (Dol)     23
          Wkst/Wkst-Pkst     25
          dtype: int64
```

Visualizations

You can use Python to create a bar chart based upon the lithofacies size; this makes it a bit easier to understand as shown in the following screenshot:

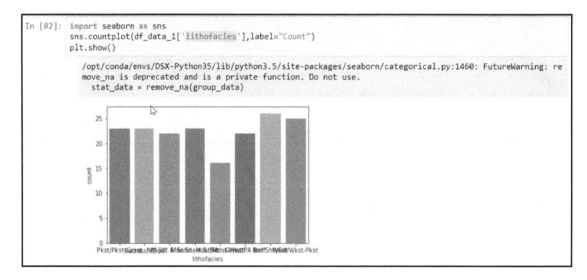

```
In [82]:  import seaborn as sns
          sns.countplot(df_data_1['lithofacies'],label="Count")
          plt.show()
```

/opt/conda/envs/DSX-Python35/lib/python3.5/site-packages/seaborn/categorical.py:1460: FutureWarning: re
move_na is deprecated and is a private function. Do not use.
  stat_data = remove_na(group_data)

Box plotting

Often used in performing explanatory data analysis, a box plot is a type of graph that is used to show and understand the shape of a distribution, its central value, and its variability. Seeing a box plot for each numeric variable in our well log data will give you a better idea of the distribution of the input variables as shown in the following screenshot:

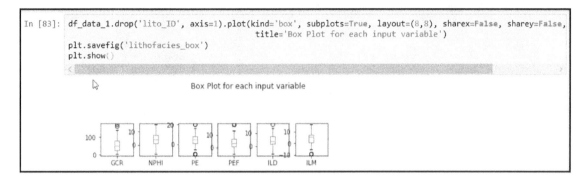

Histogram

A **histogram** is used to graphically recap and display the distribution of data points within a dataset.

Using the following Python code, we can now try a histogram for each numeric input value within our data (GCR, ILD, ILM, NPHI, PE, and PEF):

```python
import pylab as pl
df_data_1.drop('lito_ID' ,axis=1).hist(bins=30, figsize=(10,10))
pl.suptitle("Histogram for each numeric input variable")
plt.savefig('lithofacies_hist')
plt.show()
```

This gives you the following output:

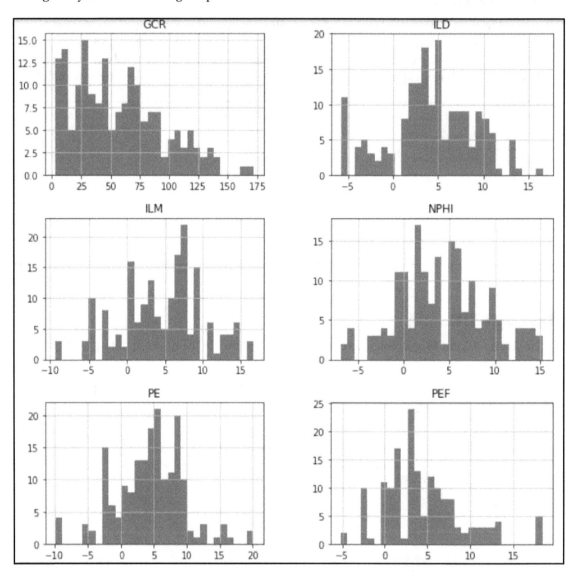

Once a histogram is generated from the data, the first question that is usually asked is whether the shape of the histogram is normal. A characteristic of a **normal distribution** (of data), s, is that it is symmetrical. This means that if the distribution is cut in half, each side will be the mirror of the other, forming a bell-shaped curve, as shown in the following screenshot:

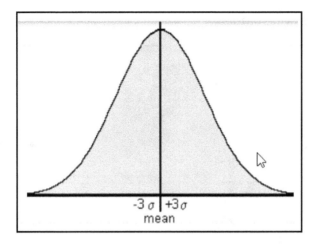

From our generated histograms, perhaps the **NPHI** data point comes the closest to showing a normal distribution.

The scatter matrix

A **scatter matrix** is another common analysis tool as it include several pairwise scatter plots of variables presented in a matrix format. It is also used to verify if variables are correlated and whether the correlation is positive or negative.

The following code can be used to experiment with this type of visualization:

```
from pandas.tools.plotting import scatter_matrix
from matplotlib import cm
feature_names = [ 'GCR', 'NPHI', 'PE', 'ILD', 'ILM']
X = df_data_1[feature_names]
y = df_data_1['lito_ID']
cmap = cm.get_cmap('gnuplot')
scatter = pd.plotting.scatter_matrix(X, c = y, marker = 'o', s=40,
hist_kwds={'bins':15}, figsize=(9,9), cmap = cmap)
plt.suptitle('Scatter-matrix for each input variable')
plt.savefig('lithofacies_scatter_matrix')
```

This gives you the following output:

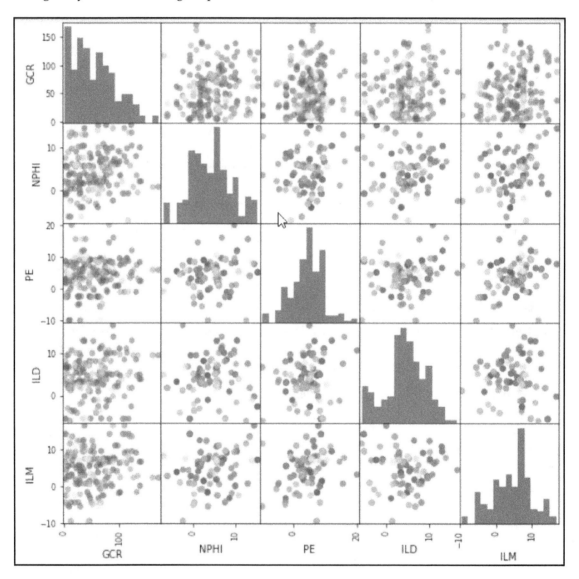

A scatter plot attempts to reveal relationships or associations between variables (called a correlation). Refer to the following link to learn more about scatter plots:

https://mste.illinois.edu/courses/ci330ms/youtsey/scatterinfo.html

Looking at the scatter plot generated from our log data (shown in the preceding screenshot), I really don't see any specific or direct correlations between the data.

At this point, you may continue performing a deep dive into the data, perform some reforming or aggregations, or even perhaps go back to the original source (of the data) and request additional or new data.

In the interest of time, for this exercise, we will assume that we will use what data we have and move on to creating and testing various modeling algorithms.

Training the classifier

`scikit-learn` library can be used to code machine learning classifier and is the only Python library which has four-step modeling pattern.

 Refer to the following link for more information about `sckit-learn`: http://www.jmlr.org/papers/volume12/pedregosa11a/pedregosa11a.pdf.

The coding process of implementing the `scikit-learn` model applies to various classifiers within `sklearn`, such as decision trees, **k-nearest neighbors** (**KNN**), and more. We will look at a few of these classifiers here, using our well logging data.

The first step in using Scikit to build a model is to create training and test datasets and apply scaling, using the following lines of Python code:

```
from sklearn.model_selection import train_test_split
X_train, X_test, y_train, y_test = train_test_split(X, y, random_state=0)
from sklearn.preprocessing import MinMaxScaler
scaler = MinMaxScaler()
X_train = scaler.fit_transform(X_train)
X_test = scaler.transform(X_test)
```

Now that we have created a training dataset, we can proceed with building our various types of machine learning models using that data. Typically, in a particular machine learning project, you will have some idea as to the type of machine learning algorithm that you'll want to use, but perhaps not. Either way, you want to verify the performance of your selected algorithm(s).

The following sections show the Python commands which with to create models based using the `scikit-learn` module.

Building a logistic regression model

Regression analysis is used to understand which of the independent variables (our features: GCR, NPHI, PE, ILD, and ILM) are related to the dependent variable; that is, the type of lithofacies.

The following lines of Python code create a logistic regression classifier model and print its accuracy statistics:

```
                build a Logistic Regression model

In [16]:   from sklearn.linear_model import LogisticRegression
           logreg = LogisticRegression()
           logreg.fit(X_train, y_train)
           print('Accuracy of Logistic regression classifier on training set: {:.2f}'
               .format(logreg.score(X_train, y_train)))
           print('Accuracy of Logistic regression classifier on test set: {:.2f}'
               .format(logreg.score(X_test, y_test)))

           Accuracy of Logistic regression classifier on training set: 0.15
           Accuracy of Logistic regression classifier on test set: 0.00
```

Building a KNN model

The KNN algorithm is a simple, supervised machine learning algorithm that can also be used for classification and regression problems.

The following lines of Python code create a KNN classifier model and print its accuracy statistics:

```
                build a K-Nearest Neighbors model

In [18]:   from sklearn.neighbors import KNeighborsClassifier
           knn = KNeighborsClassifier()
           knn.fit(X_train, y_train)
           print('Accuracy of K-NN classifier on training set: {:.2f}'
               .format(knn.score(X_train, y_train)))
           print('Accuracy of K-NN classifier on test set: {:.2f}'
               .format(knn.score(X_test, y_test)))

           Accuracy of K-NN classifier on training set: 0.27
           Accuracy of K-NN classifier on test set: 0.00
```

Building a Gaussian Naive Bayes model

Given the class variable, all Naive Bayes classifiers infer that the value of a particular feature in the data is independent of the value of any other feature.

The following lines of Python code create a **Gaussian Naive Bayes** (**GaussianNB**) classifier model and print its accuracy statistics:

```
                Gaussian Naive Bayes

In [32]:   from sklearn.naive_bayes import GaussianNB
           gnb = GaussianNB()
           gnb.fit(X_train, y_train)
           print('Accuracy of GNB classifier on training set: {:.2f}
               .format(gnb.score(X_train, y_train)))
           print('Accuracy of GNB classifier on test set: {:.2f}'
               .format(gnb.score(X_test, y_test)))

           Accuracy of GNB classifier on training set: 0.99
           Accuracy of GNB classifier on test set: 0.00
```

Building a support vector machine model

A **support vector machine** (**SVM**) is a supervised learning model with associated learning algorithms that analyze data used for classification and regression analysis.

The following lines of Python code create an SVM classifier model and print its accuracy statistics:

```
                buid a Support Vector Machine model

In [25]:   from sklearn.svm import SVC
           svm = SVC()
           svm.fit(X_train, y_train)
           print('Accuracy of SVM classifier on training set: {:.2f}'
               .format(svm.score(X_train, y_train)))
           print('Accuracy of SVM classifier on test set: {:.2f}'
               .format(svm.score(X_test, y_test)))

           Accuracy of SVM classifier on training set: 0.99
           Accuracy of SVM classifier on test set: 0.00
```

Building a decision tree model

A decision tree is a decision support tool that uses a tree-like model of decisions and their possible consequences, including chance event outcomes, resource costs, and utility.

The following lines of Python code create a decision tree classifier mode and print its accuracy statistics:

```
Build a Decision Tree model

In [96]:  from sklearn.tree import DecisionTreeClassifier
          clf = DecisionTreeClassifier().fit(X_train, y_train)
          print('Accuracy of Decision Tree classifier on training set: {:.2f}'
              .format(clf.score(X_train, y_train)))
          print('Accuracy of Decision Tree classifier on test set: {:.2f}'
              .format(clf.score(X_test, y_test)))
          print(clf)

          Accuracy of Decision Tree classifier on training set: 0.99
          Accuracy of Decision Tree classifier on test set: 0.00
          DecisionTreeClassifier(class_weight=None, criterion='gini', max_depth=None,
                      max_features=None, max_leaf_nodes=None,
                      min_impurity_decrease=0.0, min_impurity_split=None,
                      min_samples_leaf=1, min_samples_split=2,
                      min_weight_fraction_leaf=0.0, presort=False, random_state=None,
                      splitter='best')
```

Summing them up

Again, if we were working a real project, this step or phase (of the project) would include a much deeper review of each model's performance results and, perhaps, would require the decision to even return back to the data exploration and transformation phase. However, for the sake of time, we'll move forward.

Since we've now seen some simple ways for creating and, at least, superficially judging each model's performance (as far as accuracy), we will move on to the last section of this chapter and look at an example of visualizing a selected model using Python commands.

Evaluating the classifier

Reviewing the outputs printed after each model build, we should notice that the decision tree model has one of the best results:

```
Accuracy of Decision Tree classifier on training set: 0.99
Accuracy of Decision Tree classifier on test set: 0.00
```

A disclaimer of sorts

Typically, we would spend much more time evaluating and verifying the performance of a selected model (and continually training it), but again, you get the general idea (there is plenty of due diligence work to do!), and our goals are more around demonstrating the steps in building an end-to-end machine learning solution using IBM Watson Studio and its resources.

With that in mind, we will now use some Python code to create some visualizations of our models.

Understanding decision trees

Decision tree algorithms are very commonly-used supervised learning algorithm models for classification and regression tasks. In this section, we will show how you can visualize decision tree classifiers to better understand their logic.

Decision tree classifiers build a sequence of simple if/else rulings on data through the use of which they can then predict the target value.

Decision trees are usually simpler to interpret because of their structure and the ability we have to visualize the modeled tree, using modules such as the `sklearn export_graphviz` function.

The following standard Python code can be used to visualize the decision tree model that we previously built in our notebook:

```
!pip install graphviz
from sklearn.tree import DecisionTreeClassifier, export_graphviz
from sklearn import tree
from sklearn.datasets import load_wine
from IPython.display import SVG
from graphviz import Source
from IPython.display import display

# feature matrix
feature_names = [ 'GCR', 'NPHI', 'PE', 'ILD', 'ILM']
X = df_data_1[feature_names]

# target vector
y = df_data_1['lithofacies']

# print dataset description
estimator = DecisionTreeClassifier()
```

```
estimator.fit(X, y)

graph = Source(tree.export_graphviz(estimator, out_file=None
    , feature_names=labels
    , filled = True))
display(SVG(graph.pipe(format='svg')))
```

 The sample code can be found at https://towardsdatascience.com/ interactive-visualization-of-decision-trees-with-jupyter-widgets-ca15dd312084.

The following screenshot shows the code executed in our notebook and the graphical output it creates (although this is difficult to fit into a single screenshot):

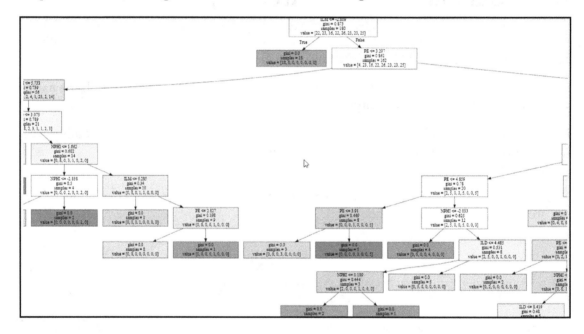

Very seldom does one allow.

Summary

In this chapter, we introduced a real-world use case in the evaluation of well drilling logs to classify lithofacies.

We loaded a sample file and performed various profiling and visualization exercises comparing Watson profiles, as well as using Python commands within a notebook. Finally, we used specialized Python libraries to build various types of models and then presented a graph of a supervised machine learning algorithm.

In the next chapter, we will build a cloud-based, multibiometric identity authentication platform.

10
Building a Cloud-Based Multibiometric Identity Authentication Platform

In this chapter, using **IBM Watson Studio**, we will walk through the construction of a functioning cloud-based *human* identification system using **biometric traits**. We will first introduce biometrics and consider what we mean by biometric data. Then, we will explain the types of preprocessing needed for each biometric. Additionally, we will learn about the process of how to extract meaningful features from biometric data. Lastly, we will cover the concepts behind **multimodal data fusion**.

The following topics will be covered in this chapter:

- Understanding biometrics
- Exploring biometric data
- Feature extraction
- Biometric recognition
- Multimodal fusion
- Our example

Understanding biometrics

If we start by breaking down the word itself, **biometrics** is derived from the Greek words **bio** (life) and **metrics** (to measure), and so biometric relates to the application of statistical analysis to biological data.

Biometric verification is defined as the process by which someone can be uniquely identified by evaluating one (or more) distinguishing biological traits.

Unique identifiers typically used in the process of biometric verification include the following:

- Fingerprints
- Hand geometry
- Earlobe geometry
- Retina/iris patterns
- Voice (waves)
- DNA
- Signatures

For those of us who are *Forensic Files* fans, one of the oldest forms of biometric verification is fingerprinting. You can refer to the article in the following link for more details about how the first forensic files came into implementation: `http://onin.com/fp/fphistory.html`.

Biometric verification and authentication have advanced significantly with technology advancements, such as the digitization of analog data (not to mention IBM Watson!), which now allow for practically instantaneous personal identification to take place.

While it may be quite obvious that the biometric authentication process uses physical characteristics (fingerprinting) to digitally identify (or authenticate) a person, more advanced solutions may also utilize behavioral human traits (like voice cadence) as well.

Each of these (characteristics) is considered unique to a particular individual, and, therefore, they may be used in combination (more on combining identifiers a bit later on in this chapter) to ensure greater accuracy of identification.

Making a case

Why is biometric verification such a topic of interest?

The answer is that, in an instantaneous and ever more internet-enabled world, password authentication is slow and, frankly, just not good (strong) enough.

According to recent popular opinion (*4 reasons why biometric security is the way forward*, Digitial Biometrics, AUG 2015), the following four reasons top the list as to why biometric verification is so important:

- The IoT landscape is becoming more complex
- Passwords are not strong enough
- Biometric security is more efficient
- More companies and institutions are embracing biometrics

Almost every one of us has had to create or choose a password and has been informed that the chosen phrase is weak or not strong enough. A weak password is one that is easy to detect both by humans or an automated process.

People frequently use guessable passwords such as the names of their children or their house number (so that they won't forget the password) but the simpler or the weaker the **password**, the easier it will be to detect or duplicate.

Biometric authentication is a more effective way to prove identity or authenticate someone since it cannot be simulated or replicated, and it is nearly impossible for hackers to manipulate the authentication process, even with the use of malware and other viruses.

Popular use cases

Some of the *current* and practical areas where biometric authentication technologies are at work include the following:

- Border and immigration
- Workforce management
- Criminal identification
- Airport security
- Time-keeping and attendance
- Law enforcement
- Access control and **Single Sign On (SSO)**
- Banking

All indications are that this technology will continue to grow and mature as apparent in the article *Use of Biometrics Across the Globe* by John Trader of M2SYS Technology (`http://www.m2sys.com/blog/biometric-hardware/top-5-uses-biometrics-across-globe/amp/`).

From a financial perspective, according to the **Security Industry Association** (**SIA**), the market for electronic access controls in the USA alone is expected to top 4.47 billion in 2019 (up from just over 3 billion in 2014).

To further make the case for biometric authentication, an online article, *Millennials Accelerating the End of the Password Era* (January 29, 2018, by Limor Kessem), we see that although password use is not popular, when logging into applications *security* is the biggest (by far) concern for users (`https://securityintelligence.com/new-ibm-study-consumers-weigh-in-on-biometrics-authentication-and-the-future-of-identity/`).

Privacy concerns

With the convenience and security of biometrics comes a concern for privacy. For any biometric authentication solution to work, it requires a database containing the relevant information for each individual to be identified and authorized by the system. This means that every user's biometric signature would have to be recorded so that the solution could use the information to verify each person's identity. The safekeeping, ethical use, and governance of this information becomes critical.

In addition to the aforementioned, by their nature, biometric systems also collect more information than just the users' fingerprints, retinal patterns, or other biometric data. At a basic level, most systems will record the time and place a person is at the time of an authentication. This also leads to the concern over how and where this information could potentially be used.

Some final words on this particular topic: a recent court ruling emphasized the importance of providing (prior) notice of biometric data collection and use. Be careful when dealing with biometrics: violating the law will most likely result in you or your company being sued.

Components of a biometric authentication solution

The components that make up a biometric authentication solution include the following:

- A sensor or other device to capture the biometrics
- Data storage to save the biometrics
- A machine learning matching algorithm(s)
- A decision processor or how to handle the results of the previous three

In the next section, we will start exploring biometric data.

Exploring biometric data

After reading the preceding sections of this chapter and, hopefully, understanding the purpose and opportunity of using biometrics data within a solution, the next step is a walk-through, conceptually at least, for building the solution.

When using biometric information for authentication, we would see the following:

- **Collection of biometric data**: This step uses some sort of input device to capture biometric data. The input of this information is typically referred to as biometric scanning. This scanning may be a fingerprint, the iris of the eye, vocal prompts, or other forms of biometric scanning (quite often photographs are the first biometric form that is used, since photographs are easy to understand and manage).
- **Conversion, labeling, and storage of biometric data**: The data that is collected through scanning must then be converted into a digital format and saved in a database and appropriately labeled. This database stores the biometric data of individuals that will need to be authorized by the solution.
- **Selection and configuration of an ML algorithm**: A **matching algorithm** is used to compare newly scanned data to data that is stored and labeled within the digital database. Upon a match, the individual is authenticated, and then decision logic is used to decide what the next step will be, such as granting access to a system or location.

Specific Individual identification

So, biometric identification involves determining the identity of a specific person by comparing an individual presented (or scanned) **biometric signature** with that which is already cataloged in the solutions database and making a decision: does it or doesn't it match? This can be seen in the following diagram:

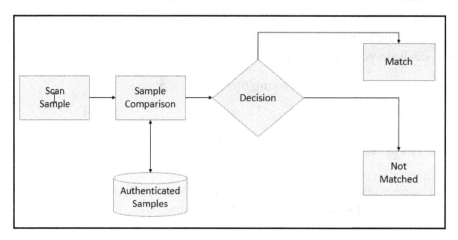

A biometric signature can be an item obtained from the individual such as the following:

- A photo of their face
- A record of their voice
- An image of their fingerprint

Keep in mind that **biometric data** is a general term used to refer to any data that is created during a **biometric scanning process**.

In addition to the previously mentioned, this biometric data may also include any samples, models, fingerprints, similarity scores, and all verification or identification data including the individual's name and demographics.

Also included in the individual's signature can be palm veins, face recognition, DNA, palm print, hand geometry, iris recognition, retina, and odor/scent. Further, **behavioral characteristics** that are related to the pattern of behavior of an individual (for example, his or her a gait or typing rhythm) may also be part of the biometric database.

It should also be of note that, since biometric data is digital in format, it can be efficiently processed by computer systems and easily encrypted as a safeguard against unethical manipulation and use by unauthorized persons.

Another point is the submission of a single set of biometric samples to a biometric system for identification or verification is referred to as an attempt. For obvious reasons, solutions typically allow only a single attempt to identify or verify an individual. Attempts made by individuals who do not have a cataloged biometric signature previously scanned and cataloged within the solutions database will fail authentication. This is significant since it reduces the amount of data needing to be scanned and cataloged for the solution to work: you only need to establish digital signatures for those individuals that do need to be authenticated and granted access.

The Challenge of Biometric Data Use

Collecting, cataloging, and using biometric data can be a challenge. This form of data is, like most data, subject to uncertainty and variation. Perhaps unique to biometric data, we see that this information may be affected by changes in an individual's age, environmental influences, disease, stress, occupational factors, training and prompting, intentional alterations, sociocultural aspects of the situation in which the presentation occurs, changes in human interface with the system, and so on.

As a result, each interaction or attempt of an individual may be associated with different biometric information.

Sample sizing

In Chapter 8, *Creating a Facial Expression Platform on IBM Cloud* , we constructed an expression analysis model using facial images for the model to train on and use to detect human emotions: happiness, sadness, and anger. In that exercise, we chose a sample size for each emotion of just 11 images:

In that exercise, the sample size (11) was sufficient since the goal was to prove our concept. Obviously, the bigger the sample size the more accurate the model.

A **biometric authentication** solution works on the same premise; however, rather than detecting emotion from an attempt, the model will compare the *scanned* image to its cataloged database, looking for a match. Since the scanned image will not be one that is in the database, the matching algorithm must compare the databased images and detect the individual based upon its facial recognition and evaluation logics. If there is simply one image of each authenticated user within the database, the margin for error increases. Therefore, how many images (for each user) are needed? What is the optimal sample size (for a biometric authentication solution) to be used?

Biometric system performance is typically evaluated by collecting biometric templates (or biometric signatures) from n different subjects, and, for convenience, acquiring multiple instances of that biometric (for example, photographs) for each of the n subjects.

Unfortunately, you most likely found that there isn't much work available to date on constructing confidence regions based on the **Receiver Operating Characteristic (ROC)** curve for validating the claimed performance levels and determining the required number of biometric samples needed to establish confidence regions of prespecified width for the ROC curve.

 ROC is widely used to determine how a predictive model can distinguish between true positives and negatives. To accomplish this task, a model needs to correctly predict not only a positive as a positive but also a negative as a negative.

Feature extraction

Biometric feature extraction (also sometimes named minutia extraction) refers to the process by which established *key* features of a sample are selected or enhanced for more efficient processing. Typically, the process of feature extraction relies on a set of algorithms that varies depending on the type (face image or fingerprints, for example) of biometric identification used.

Biometric authentication is the matching of samples that have been converted (previously or upon attempt) from, for example, an image of a biometric trait into a searchable set of data. This conversion is the process known as feature extraction.

If you look for example of how feature extraction fundamentally works, you see that it depends upon the type of sample, but is, for the most part, quite easy to conceptualize. You can head over to the following link to know more on how a biometric matching works: `http://devtechnology.com/2013/11/emerging-biometric-technology-revocable-biometric-features/`.

 Some other examples of biometric feature extraction can also be referred to the article in the following link: `http://arindamcctvaccesscontrol.blogspot.com/2010/05/access-control-index-terminology.html`.

Biometric recognition

A biometric recognition and ultimately a successful authentication depend upon the robustness of the selected machine learning algorithm used within the solution but also on (as we discussed in the *Feature extraction* section of this chapter) the sample size.

In addition to these requirements, it is important to consider the quality of the samples as well as the type. Poor image quality, for example, can significantly impact the accuracy of a biometric authentication. We also briefly mentioned using **behavioral traits** as part of a biometric signature.

Generally speaking though, **physiological characteristics** (such as a fingerprint or facial picture, for instance) are always the most static, showing little dissimilarity over time, while **behavioral characteristics** (that is, a gait or cadence) can and usually do experience variations, and can be prejudiced by external factors or by particular emotional conditions such as stress or strong psychological impacts.

Interesting **behavioral characteristics** already in use by some biometric authentication solutions include vocal imprints, writing and/or typing style, movements of the body, the style and the trend of walk, and so on.

Multimodal fusion

Most simply put, the more gates surrounding an individual's property, the more secure it will be, since we would need to possess the ability to successfully pass more than a single test to proceed. The same applies to any system or solution that makes a decision to proceed based upon the outcome of a test (match or no-match). Adding additional tests produces additional outcomes and additional decisions based upon those outcomes.

Biometric authentication solutions are typically considered unimodal (conducts only a single test) or multimodal (conducts more than a single test):

- **Multimodal biometric authentication**: This describes an implemented solution that utilizes multiple biometric indicators for identifying the authenticated individuals, such as a photo/image and a signature. A successful match of both biometrics is required to succeed.
- **Unimodal biometric authentication**: This describes a solution that utilizes only a single level of authentication, such as only a photo/image or a signature. In this case, if the solution matches successfully to the biometric (for example, and image) the attempt is successful.

Our example

Now that we have an idea and understanding of just what a biometric authentication solution is and how it works, we will try to build a simple but actually working prototype using the same **IBM Watson Visual Recognition service** we used in Chapter 8, *Creating a Facial Expression Platform on IBM Cloud*, as well as that project as a guide for our new solution.

 As a reminder, the IBM Watson Visual Recognition service understands the image content out-of-the-box (we demonstrated this in our Chapter 8, *Creating a Facial Expression Platform on IBM Cloud* project). The pretrained models provided enable you to analyze images for objects, faces, colors, food, explicit content, and other subjects for insights into your visual content. We successfully used the service to detect faces and then determine expressions.

Premise

The general premise will be to clone our Chapter 8, *Creating a Facial Expression Platform on IBM Cloud*, project and create a class or classes to be used as a simple biometric signature for myself; one loaded with a dozen images of, well, my face, as well as a negative class loaded with a dozen images of random faces (none will be of me).

In addition, there will be at least one other class, designed to be a biometric signature of another individual. So we expect that, in this chapter's project, we will have the following three classes:

- Jim class
- Individual two or other classes
- Negative class

The final step will be to use a mobile device to take several photos of myself and others and, without preparation or any processing of the images, submit the facial images to our project and record the results: matched or not matched. These image submissions will be considered our attempts for biometric authentication.

Perhaps to test the project fairly, we will need to be sure to submit several images of myself (none of which would be part of the model's class definitions my biometric signature) and several faces that are not mine and record the results of each submission.

Finally, we will evaluate and record the results.

Data preparation

Straightaway, we need to have a sample of 10 images of my face. The images should be of reasonable quality and, for best results, close-up photos taken over a period of time so that the algorithm can have some accounting for variances in my appearance.

 If you have forgotten, you can review Chapter 8, *Creating a Facial Expression Platform on IBM Cloud*, for the specific file image requirements.

Here are the images that will be used to create my biometric signature:

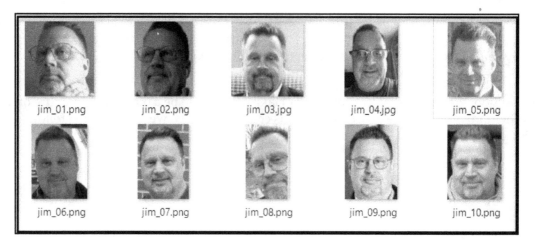

Next, we need to establish a biometric signature (with the same size sample) for another individual:

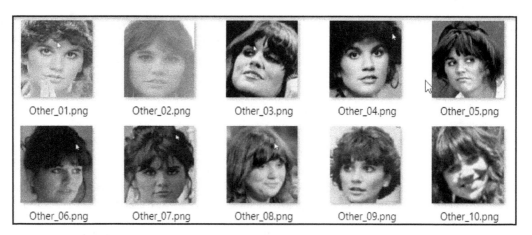

Finally, the negative class of 10 random faces (of course, borrowed from our project) needs to be set:

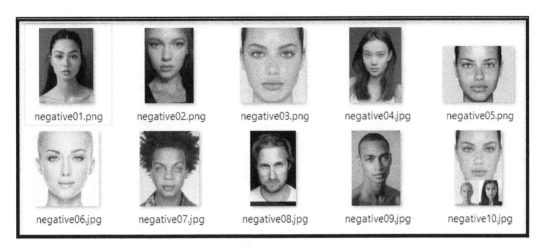

A reminder from Watson docs: The **create a classifier** call requires that you provide at least two example ZIP files: two positive examples files or one positive and one negative file. The negative examples defines what the updated classifier is not. It is not used to create a class within the created classifier. Negative example files will contain images **that do not match the subject of any of the positive examples**. In a single call, there can be only one single example specified.

Project setup

Once again, we will assume that we have already created a new IBM Watson Studio project and now (as in Chapter 8, *Creating a Facial Expression Platform on IBM Cloud*) add a new visual recognition model by going to the **Assets** tab and under **Models**, click on **New Visual Recognition model** (you can go back to Chapter 8, *Creating a Facial Expression Platform on IBM Cloud*, for a quick review).

Just like in Chapter 8, *Creating a Facial Expression Platform on IBM Cloud*, once the model is created (it should take only a few moments), you can drag and drop the image .zip files we prepared in the preceding sections of this chapter.

This will upload the image files to **Cloud Object Storage** (**COO**), making them available to be used in our project (as shown in the following screenshot):

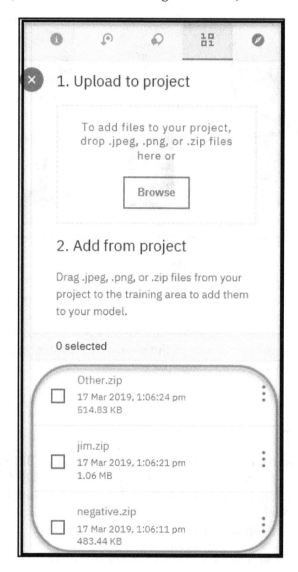

From the **Default Custom Model** screen (in the following screenshot), we are ready to build our model classes:

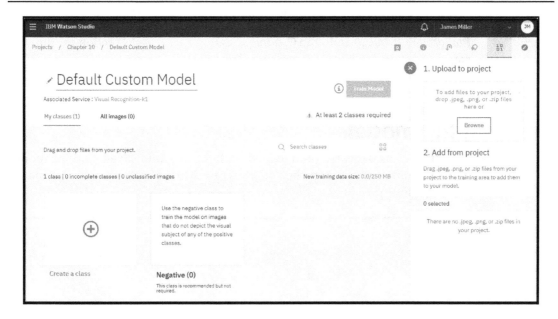

Creating classes

You can now click on the **Create a class** button (shown on the bottom left in the following screenshot) to create both the **Jim** and **Other** classes (remember, the **Negative** class is already created for you):

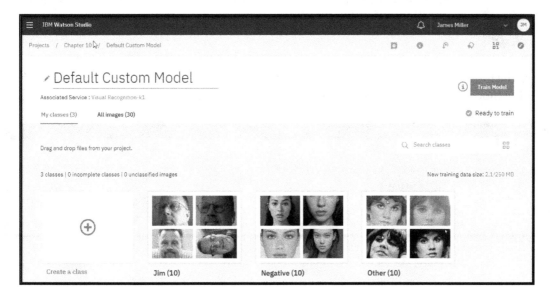

Again, you can refer back to Chapter 8, *Creating a Facial Expression Platform on IBM Cloud,* to the *Creating Classes for Our Model* section for the step-by-step instructions for creating classes.

Training the model

Once we have our three classes created (and loaded with images) and saved, and the model status shows **Ready to train**, we can then click on the **Train Model** button to start training the model on the images we provided:

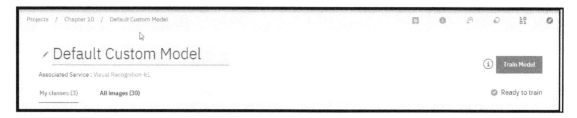

Once more, this is a small model with only 30 training images; the training process will take less than 5 or 10 minutes. Part of the beauty of using IBM Watson and services is that many of the "detailed tasks" like creating model definitions and training a model is simply a "button click". To learn more about training a visual recognition model, you can visit:

https://dataplatform.cloud.ibm.com/docs/content/wsj/analyze-data/visual-recognition-train.html?linkInPage=true

Once the model training has been completed and you notice (see the following screenshot) that the model status says **Trained**, you can proceed:

Just as we did in `Chapter 8`, *Creating a Facial Expression Platform on IBM Cloud,* to test and validate our model, we can upload images in the **Test** area of the **Default Custom Model** page, as shown in the following screenshot:

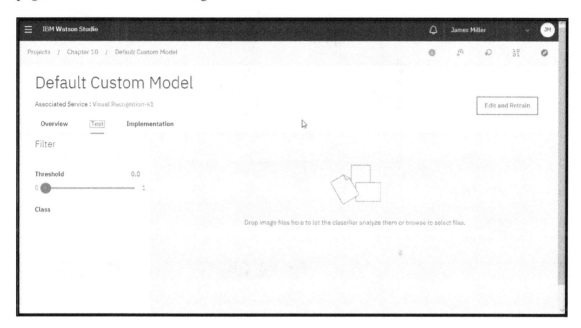

Testing our project

Just as we have planned, the final step of our project exercise is to use a mobile device to take several photos of myself and others and, without preparation of the images, submit the facial images to our project for authentication and record the results: matched or not matched.

Using my smartphone, I took the following three head shots. I tried to capture a variation in lighting and expression:

In addition, as we stated earlier, to test our project fairly, we need to submit several images of faces that are not mine and record the results of each submission as well.

For these test subjects, I collected the following:

Now it's testing time!

As we can see in the following screenshot, I submitted the first four images: Jim, Jim, Jim, and other. The model correctly authenticated each image that was submitted:

That's pretty good, right? Now we can submit the fourth and final image (*not* Jim and *not* other) and zoom in on all of the scores:

Guidelines for good training

We have now created a simple biometric authentication proof of concept using IBM Watson Studio and the IBM Watson Visual Recognition service. It works but of course this is not ready for deployment. There are many things to consider before a model is ready for deployment and production use. For example, guidelines provided with the Visual Recognition service state that it is best practice to include at least 50 positive images *per class* before you can begin to realistically assess your training results.

Other recommendations provided include the following:

- Assuming similar quality and content for your training data, more training images generally provide more accurate results than fewer images.
- 150 to 200 images per `.zip` file provides the best balance between processing time and accuracy. More than 200 images will increase the time and the accuracy, but with diminishing returns for the amount of time it takes.

Implementation

To the right of the **Test** tab is the **Implementation** tab (shown in the following screenshot). From here, you can see the the code snippets provided for you by Watson to classify images against the model you just built:

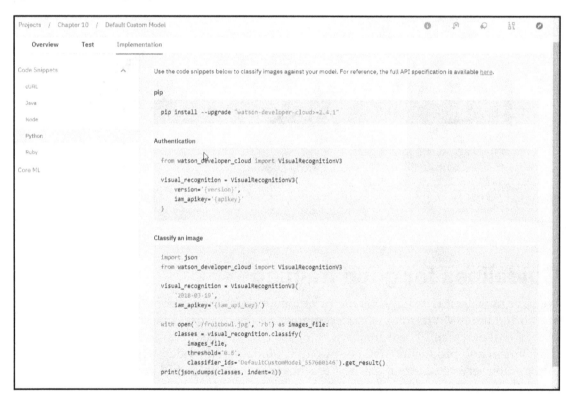

For reference, the full API specification you will need to deploy the model is available here: `https://cloud.ibm.com/apidocs/visual-recognition`.

Summary

In this chapter, we introduced and discussed collecting and using biometric data in a biometric authentication solution, how such a solution works as well as feature extraction (in regard to biometric data solutions) was the idea of multimodal fusion. Finally, we expanded the expression detection and analysis solution from `Chapter 8`, *Creating a Facial Expression Platform on IBM Cloud*, again using the IBM Watson Visual Recognition service, to create a working biometric authentication solution proof of concept.

The next chapter concludes this book with an overview of what we have covered. The chapter will also shed some light on some of the practical considerations related to developing machine learning systems on the cloud with IBM Watson Studio.

Another Book You May Enjoy

If you enjoyed this book, you may be interested in these other books by Packt:

IBM Watson Projects
James Miller

ISBN: 978-1-78934-371-7

- Build a smart dialog system with cognitive assistance solutions
- Design a text categorization model and perform sentiment analysis on social media datasets
- Develop a pattern recognition application and identify data irregularities smartly
- Analyze trip logs from a driving services company to determine profit
- Provide insights into an organization's supply chain data and processes
- Create personalized recommendations for retail chains and outlets
- Test forecasting effectiveness for better sales prediction strategies

Leave a review - let other readers know what you think

Please share your thoughts on this book with others by leaving a review on the site that you bought it from. If you purchased the book from Amazon, please leave us an honest review on this book's Amazon page. This is vital so that other potential readers can see and use your unbiased opinion to make purchasing decisions, we can understand what our customers think about our products, and our authors can see your feedback on the title that they have worked with Packt to create. It will only take a few minutes of your time, but is valuable to other potential customers, our authors, and Packt. Thank you!

Index